THE THEATRE OF ROBERT EDMOND JONES

THE THEATRE

With contributions by

JOHN MASON BROWN

MARY HALL FURBER

KENNETH MACGOWAN

JO MIELZINER

DONALD OENSLAGER

LEE SIMONSON

STARK YOUNG

Illustrated with over fifty plates

OF ROBERT EDMOND JONES

EDITED AND WITH A CHRONOLOGY BY
RALPH PENDLETON

WESLEYAN UNIVERSITY PRESS : MIDDLETOWN : CONNECTICUT

Out of the manifold contacts of my experience the image of a new theatre has gradually formed itself—a theatre not yet made with hands. I look forward to this ideal theatre and work toward it.

ROBERT EDMOND JONES
from *The Dramatic Imagination*

TABLE OF CONTENTS

STARK YOUNG   Robert Edmond Jones: A Note   3

MARY HALL FURBER   The Scene: New Hampshire, U.S.A.   7

LEE SIMONSON   Legacy   14

JO MIELZINER   Practical Dreams   20

Plates   *begin facing page* 28

DONALD OENSLAGER   "Settings by Robert Edmond Jones"   131

KENNETH MACGOWAN   Jones as Director and Film Designer   139

RALPH PENDLETON   Robert Edmond Jones: A Chronology   144

JOHN MASON BROWN   L'Envoi   185

A Footnote to This Edition   187

Index of Productions   189

LIST OF ILLUSTRATIONS

Robert Edmond Jones *by Leo Mielziner*   *facing page* 10

Plates

THE CENCI	28
THE MAN WHO MARRIED A DUMB WIFE	30
REDEMPTION	32
THE BIRTHDAY OF THE INFANTA: Scene II	34
KING RICHARD III	36
MACBETH: *The Banquet Scene*	38
MACBETH: *The Sleepwalking Scene*	40
SWORDS	42
PELLÉAS ET MÉLISANDE	44
HAMLET: *The Madness of Ophelia*	46
HAMLET: *The Burial of Ophelia*	48
THE KINGDOM OF SANCHO PANZA	50
AT THE GATEWAY	52
DESIRE UNDER THE ELMS	54
THE FOUNTAIN	56
MUCH ADO ABOUT NOTHING	58
SKYSCRAPERS	60
THE HOUSE OF WOMEN	62
LA GIOCONDA	64
FAUST	66
MACHINAL	68

YOLANDA OF CYPRUS *facing page*	70
THE GREEN PASTURES: *The Lord and Noah*	72
THE GREEN PASTURES: *The Prayer of Moses*	74
THE GREEN PASTURES: *The Vision of Hezdrel*	76
LE PREZIOSE RIDICOLE	78
OEDIPUS REX	80
MOURNING BECOMES ELECTRA	82
NIGHT OVER TAOS	84
CAMILLE: *Auteuil*	86
CAMILLE: *Marguerite's Bedroom*	88
OTHELLO: *The Duel*	90
OTHELLO: *A Bedchamber*	92
THE PHILADELPHIA STORY	94
PELLÉAS ET MÉLISANDE	96
THE BARBER OF SEVILLE	98
KING RICHARD III: *The Vision of the Crown*	100
KING RICHARD III: *The Ghost of Lady Anne*	102
THE OLD FOOLISHNESS	104
THE LORDS OF THE WEST	106
KING HENRY VIII: *Buckingham's Farewell*	108
KING HENRY VIII: *Blackfriars*	110
KING HENRY VIII: *The Queen's Apartment*	112
KING HENRY VIII: *The Coronation*	114

LUTE SONG: *A Curtain*   *facing page* 116
LUTE SONG: *The Street of Shops*   118
LUTE SONG: *The Blue Pavilion*   120
THE ICEMAN COMETH   122
A TOUCH OF THE POET   124
MACBETH   126
MACBETH   128

For the Production of LUTE SONG
Set Design: *The Blue Pavilion*   *page* 132
Painter's Elevation: *Basic Setting*   133

Painter's Elevation: *Detail of Screen*   *page* 134
Working Drawing: *Garden Stone*   135
Ground Plan   136
Working Drawing: *Buddha* (detail)   137
Costume Sketch: *Property Men*   137
Performance Photographs   138

Several line drawings by Robert Edmond Jones
are reproduced in the Chronology
beginning on page 149

PREFACE

THE FIRST HALF of the twentieth century confronted the American theatre with a wide range of exceedingly complex problems: the assimilation of the European techniques of "The New Stagecraft," the development of native dramatists, the maturing of the motion picture as a separate medium, the encouragement of experimental and educational theatre, the search for new ways of fusing the visual and musical components of opera and ballet. To the solution of these problems—and so many others!—Robert Edmond Jones contributed richly during the long and astonishing career which is the subject of this volume.

Mr. Young, whose active career as a theatre critic coincides so closely with the active career of Jones himself, contributes the first chapter—and most appropriately so, for no critic of the period understood more clearly the goals which Jones had set for himself. Mrs. Furber, friend of Jones and of the Jones family for many years, presents biographical material which has not previously been available and which will put an end to the legend of the untutored farm boy who wandered almost directly from the plow to the stage of the Plymouth Theatre. Mr. Simonson, as distinguished for his contributions to theatre history as for his work as a scenic artist, discusses the concept of theatre which Jones reveals in his published essays. Mr. Mielziner and Mr. Oenslager, whose brilliant careers began with apprenticeship to Jones, record their personal memories of Jones at work; Mr. Oenslager's chapter, with its various illustrations, will help to clarify for the uninitiated the process by which a scenic artist's initial ideas are developed into the precise details of a theatrical production. Mr. Macgowan—critic, producer of plays, producer of films, theatre historian, educator, as active an agent as Jones himself for the growth of the American theatre—writes of two important phases of Jones's career concerning which far too little material has been generally available. And the book ends with a tribute by Mr. Brown, friend of Bobby Jones and of good theatre everywhere.

As compiler of the Chronology I am indebted to many correspondents, many conversations, many printed pages for hints, clues, and factual information. I am particularly indebted to Mrs. Furber, Mr. Mielziner, and Mr. Oenslager; to the late Rose Bogdanoff; to May Davenport Seymour, Curator of the Theatre Collection, Museum of the City of New York; to William Van Lennep, Curator of the Theatre Collection, Harvard College Library; to Richard E. Krug, City Librarian, and Wilbert Beck, Curator of Art and Music, Milwaukee Public Library; to Vance Kirkland, Director, School of Art, University of Denver; to Ann R. Clary, Librarian, National Headquarters, The American National Red Cross. Since my problem has been *theatrical* research, it is axiomatic that I am deeply indebted to the staff of the Theatre Collection of the New York Public Library and to the volumes of the Best Plays series edited by Burns Mantle. Finally, I should like to record my gratitude to my deceased wife, Emily White Pendleton, who was of the greatest assistance to me during the early stages of these investigations.

As editor of this book, I have had occasion to approach many, many people for information, for advice, for assistance of various kinds. The prompt and generous co-operation I have received at every hand constitutes an impressive tribute to the esteem and the affection which surround the memory of Robert Edmond Jones. For me to express a personal gratitude would be presumptuous. It is appropriate, however, for me to acknowledge the generous assistance of Mr. Mielziner and Mr. Oenslager in the selection of the illustrations for this volume, and for me to record the fact that without exception the originals of the designs selected were promptly made available by their owners for reproduction. I should record, too, that Mr. Young's remarks on THE BIRTHDAY OF THE INFANTA and MACBETH are based on the fuller discussion of these productions to be found in his *Immortal Shadows*, published in 1948 by Charles Scribner's Sons. I wish to acknowledge also the kind permission extended by Duell, Sloan & Pearce, Inc. and Theatre Arts Books of New York to print the numerous quotations from *The Dramatic Imagination* which occur in Mr. Simonson's chapter and elsewhere in this volume. I am grateful to Rinehart & Company, Inc. (formerly Farrar & Rinehart, Inc.) for permission to include the designs made by Jones for the special edition of Marc Connelly's *The Green Pastures* (copyright 1930, copyright renewed 1957 by Mr. Connelly).

In the final chapter of his book Jones wrote: "And when the curtain has fallen on the last act of our lives, if we have played our parts to the best of our ability, may we hope to hear from beyond the curtain some vibration of divine reassurance, some echo as of ghostly applause?" This book is testimony to the fact that beyond that curtain the applause of the human audience continues.

RALPH PENDLETON

Middletown, Connecticut
November 4, 1957

THE THEATRE OF ROBERT EDMOND JONES

ROBERT EDMOND JONES: A NOTE

IT GOES without saying that no art loses more in reproduction than that of the scene designer, whether the plates are from the original sketches or from stage photographs. What remains may or may not be beautiful; but obviously there is the loss in the actuality of space, for example, in the color seen under light, and in the possibilities of changes wrought by lighting. I shall do better, therefore, in writing of Robert Edmond Jones, to dwell on his inner source, as it were, on what he was trying to do, and on how, at his best, he achieved the marvellous projection of his meaning.

He once said that the scenic artist must in his mind's eye "see the high original intention of the dramatist" and strive to affirm and ennoble the art of the actors; and that he may rest content only when the curtain rising shows that these two ends are reached.

It is a better definition of himself than of his accomplishments; for in many cases his stage designs have only a most oblique relation to anything in the dramatist or the actors' ennoblement. Nevertheless it is what was back of his thoughts when he undertook a play's décor. His best creative work took place against some fiery background of excitement and revelation, and through that, time and again, he realized on the stage what was beautiful, powerful, and unique in its dramatic elevation and intense purity of mood.

The two Robert Edmond Jones designs that for me remain most unforgettable are those for the décor of MACBETH and THE BIRTHDAY OF THE INFANTA.

THE BIRTHDAY OF THE INFANTA opens with the garden courtyard of the palace. On either side the high walls rise, flat spaces with long, heavy moldings, gray varied to darker, ashen tones. At the head of the steps to the left is a door, very high, with a baroque metal awning across the top, and dark red curtains showing through the glass at the sides. A raised terrace and balustrade cross the middle stage between the two walls, and to the back there is a high iron screen, through which appear the Spanish mountains, violet hardening to blue against the cold gray-rose of the sky. All grave, and austere, and cruel, lovely, elegant, and rich. Through the great door the Infanta enters with her court and the birthday gifts. The ladies take their places, and after a mock bullfight they bring in at last the Grotesque, Pedro, the dwarf and hunchback. He is perplexed, a lonely, vague, ashen little figure as he dances to amuse the fine company. The Infanta and her court withdraw; and Pedro, eluding the guard, slips into the palace. We have then the palace vestibule, lofty and shadowed save for two great mirrors. A high door looks out on the same cold rose sky. Pedro enters, awestruck with that scene around him. In the mirrors he sees his image. For the first time he sees himself in all his ugliness and deformity. He dances a frenzied dance and falls to the floor. The Infanta comes in, calls him to dance for her, but he does not waken and she sees that he is dead. She lays her red rose on his cheek, and the court draws her away to the merriment outside.

Nowhere in Spain have I seen buildings like these in this design. But I have seen in Spain that character of sterility, of color and mass, that barbaric and cruel barrenness of sheer walls beneath the rococo and baroque and plateresque laid on the surface of them. This architecture there on the stage is not architecture in Spain or anywhere else, but a dazzling translation of architecture into theatre terms. The same is true of the costumes. They are Spanish seventeenth-century costumes seen superbly in terms of theatre.

It is the décor in this THE BIRTHDAY OF THE INFANTA that conveys much of the dramatic idea. One instance of this is where, against those iron bars and the hard mountains beyond them, the princess and her ladies in their citron color, their crimson, saffron, rose and white and gold, silver and black, sit behind the terrace balustrade and the little hunchback, in his drab and green, reaches up his lean hand toward the dazzling splendor of them. Another instance is where the little princess enters that great door and stands there under the height of it and at the top of the steps leading down, a figure like a doll, in all that relentless magnificence and order, and a symbol of the tragic puppetry of all life in the midst of time and the world's vastness.

As for MACBETH, certainly Shakespeare would not have conceived it as produced after this Robert Edmond Jones design—for that matter he would not have conceived it in the Henry Irving, or Belasco, or Winthrop Ames, or various other more familiar and plausible styles. In all seriousness I can say that for me this design for MACBETH was the most profoundly creative décor that I have ever seen in the theatre. I am using the term as Plato used it when he said: "Poetry (creation) which is the general name signifying every cause whereby anything proceeds from that which is not into that which is." There was a stage enclosed with a background of black, flat so that no light was caught to break the complete darkness of it. Drawings or photographs can give at least a suggestion, and only a suggestion, of the gold frames, or sharp gold lines, or the forms like Gothic abstractions, or however we may define them, which standing alone against the black, defined the scenes. Three great tragic masks were hung to the front, high above the action, and from them vast daggers of light poured down, crossed, pierced, flooded the action below, as in the witches' scene or the banquet. The banquet hall with its gold and light and figures moving, and above all else Lady Macbeth's robe, in which, by a hidden combination of many shades, an unheard-of intensity of red was discovered, defied any conveyance in words. Some of the scenes were like those in divers Italian fifteenth-century paintings where more than one incident is visible at the same moment: in the sleepwalking scene, for example, you saw Lady Macbeth in her long white robe coming far off to the left before you saw her enter through the pointed arch that made the doorway. The very intensity of this dramatic use of abstraction makes any effort to describe it merely futile.

If this production could have been put over with the public, it might have been a landmark in the history of the American theatre. As it turned out, the criticisms of it next day were only dull, abortive, or aggressively stupid.

Constantly in the work of Robert Edmond Jones we find the qualification and definition that arise from culture, the culture of the spirit and the culture of the mind. We have only to think of his designs for Lucrece, not drawn from classic Rome but from the Renaissance classicism in its divers styles and epochs; or of the costumes and settings out of Tiepolo, out of the Rubens Henri Quatre tapestries, figures out of Michelangelo's Sistine Chapel, out of Mantegna, color themes out of El Greco, not to mention the wonders of color and movement from Tintoretto that appeared in *Ol' Man Adam and His Chillun* when it was turned, with very few fundamental differences, into The Green Pastures. Along with this culture in other fields there went a wide and special and often highly subtle reading in many literatures.

In such instances as I have mentioned, Macbeth, The Birthday of the Infanta, and in many other scene designs by Robert Edmond Jones, there was a lustre, a high intention; and, both outwardly and at the core, there was a poetry, elusive and moving, such as we have had nowhere else in our theatre. In such instances as these consisted the truer aim of his nature, the fullness and bright drive of his mystery, when he was willing to let the quietness and romantic lure of his meditations take their way with him and to make his dream a passion.

THE SCENE: NEW HAMPSHIRE, U.S.A.

AFTER Robert Edmond Jones was graduated from Harvard and had gone to Europe where he had seen what Reinhardt was doing in Germany, he came back to design the setting for THE MAN WHO MARRIED A DUMB WIFE. From that time on, his life, his work, and his ideas were recorded by many articulate writers. But of his early years, his family and his home, little has been written beyond "he was born in a New Hampshire village"—and even that small piece of intelligence is not quite accurate.

He was born in the house which was built in 1810 as a tavern by his great-grandfather Levi Jones on Plumer's Ridge in the Township of Milton, about halfway between Portland and Portsmouth on the route of the stage coaches. The small town of Milton where Robert went to high school is four miles south.

The house does not face the road as any ordinary house would. It sprawls its length from an ample stable at the roadside through several sheds and workrooms to the kitchens, from which an entry leads into the main two-storied part, past the front door, and on into the old house. This last, three or four rooms clinging to a central chimney, had been Joseph Plumer's home since 1777. They moved it up from the field and tacked it on to the tavern. The present barn stretches its one hundred feet farther to the west. Both house and barn are painted buff, the traditional color of inns in 1800. The unshuttered windows are outlined in green, their small panes edged with "buttermilk red."

The lines of the buildings have been kept severe, like those of the house in the Jones sketch for DESIRE UNDER THE ELMS. The woods have been held well away by the open fields, the garden, and the orchard. Beyond the woods are the hills rolling into the White Mountains. That's the way it has always been.

In the house is a tiny room which may have been the office, possibly the tap-room, of the tavern. In this room, on December 12th, 1887, Emma Jane Jones gave birth to her second child, a son she named Edmond for her father, Edmond Eustis Cowell, and Robert for no known reason except that she might have thought it romantic. The time was high noon, or close enough to it so that Robert Edmond Jones could later say with peculiar satisfaction that he was born at the twelfth hour of the twelfth day of the twelfth month.

On Thanksgiving Day 1954, Robert spent the early evening, as usual, reading before the fire in this same room, and then went upstairs to the Front Chamber, the large square room which had been the Ladies' Parlor of the tavern. And in the handmade canopied bed he had known all his life he quietly died. Not the least remarkable thing about this man was that he had been born and he died, like his father Fred and his grandfather Charles before him, in this house which had meant so much to him all his life. In the years between he had gone from the house to make his name known in every part of the world where men have built a theatre.

Levi Jones had come from Lebanon, across the near border in Maine, to the Joseph Plumer farm about 1800 when he was 23, perhaps as a hired hand, and he stayed to marry Joseph's daughter Betsy. When the tavern—Plumer's Inn they called it—was built, it was Levi who managed it. Besides being a rest stop for the stages, it was a general store, meeting place, and local pub. Levi sold cheese, butter, cloth, cider, leather, fodder, and timber, all of which was produced on the place, and tea, salt, tobacco, old spirit, and molasses, which he imported. Betsy died and old Joseph died and the property came to Levi. The sign at the roadside now read JONES.

Energetic, gregarious, intelligent, Levi was a man of many interests. He may have been self-taught, but his penmanship and facility of expression are those of a trained and imaginative mind. Many of his books, small leather volumes, are still in the house. There are readers, grammars and spellers, Blackstone's Commentaries, Bibles, political speeches, rococo novels, and poetry—more poetry than one might expect. He became Town Clerk and a Justice of the Peace, he served in the War of 1812 as a major in the New Hampshire Militia, he founded a new Masonic Lodge. As he prospered, he bought up farms in the outlying districts, and when at last the tavern was closed to the public, he had become Levi Jones, Esquire. He could afford to make loans, at five per cent on "bond," to his farmer neighbors, and it might well be that Levi Jones served his community as unofficial banker and lawyer when neither was easily available otherwise.

Levi was about sixty when he married Sally Worcester Wallingford, a widow with three children. The Worcesters had come to this part of the country from Wales in 1638. Wherever a line in Robert Edmond Jones's heritage is traced, it leads to an ancestor who came from England, Scotland, or Wales in the seventeenth century to settle in New England.

Sally and Levi had one child, Charles. Although Charles was a schoolboy when Levi died, he seems to have inherited his father's social flair, and in him it became a real talent for public life. When not yet thirty he was appointed to the New Hampshire Governor's Council on which he served until his promising career was cut short by his death at the age of thirty-nine. Charles and his wife, Betsy Varney of Milton, had three children, of whom Fred was the youngest. When Betsy died not long after Charles, it was to Fred that the farm on the Ridge was given. The Civil War had brewed and flamed during Charles's lifetime, the railroad had pushed through the farm along the river, now the Jones River, and the exodus from farms to the industrial centers had begun. The security which had been intrinsic in the ownership of land was slipping away—and land, 600 acres of it, was about all young Fred had. He could not go to Harvard as his elder brother had done. He had no real training and less liking for farming as a career. But his attachment to the homestead and the land was deep. So Fred became a farmer. And he married Emma Jane Cowell.

The Cowells, like Levi's family, lived in Lebanon, across the street from the Academy where Elizabeth, Emma's mother, taught Latin, English, and drawing. Elizabeth was a Moody, one of the noted Moody family to which Ralph Waldo Emerson was proud to belong; indeed, there was an Emersonian flavor about Elizabeth in her stern daily disciplines and her reverence for learning which may have stemmed from their common Puritan ancestor. (Elizabeth was to live in the house with Emma and Fred when their children were growing up, and her influence on them was strong and salutary if not always appreciated. Robert remembered driving her in the family buggy to call on friends, her back uncompromisingly stiff, her best bonnet a-bobble with red cherries, the white bow-pin of the Women's Temperance League pinned to her bosom.)

Elizabeth had sent young Emma to Bradford Academy and then to the New England Conservatory of Music in Boston to study the piano. Emma's marked talent had earned her an opportunity to train further in Europe, but unaccountably her mother would not allow her to accept. So Emma came home to fall in love with the tall quiet boy with thick dark hair and determined jaw who lived in the rambling house on Plumer's—now Plummer's—Ridge. They were married when she was nineteen and Fred a year or two older. These two lived in the house, leaving it but briefly and then to go no great distance, for over sixty years in close companionship.

It was not easy at first for Emma, who "couldn't boil water," to master the house with its wood stoves and kerosene lamps. But she learned to cook—"like a dream," Robert said. She seemed to him to be "the beating heart of the house and if she should stop the life of the house would stop." Robert's devotion to his mother continued all her life. He wrote frequently from wherever he might be, a diary of

Robert Edmond Jones
by Leo Mielziner
Charcoal, 1925
Courtesy of Mr. Jo Mielziner

swift letters telling her about his work and his plans for more work, and he sent all the notices of his productions to her promptly. Yet Emma Jones never went to New York to see his Broadway success. Perhaps she did not need to.

Emma was a vital part of the active social life of the Ridge and the town. She gave piano lessons, and accompanied and coached the would-be singers. Some sang extraordinarily well. She had a hand in the Christmas and Graduation Day programs of the school. Nor were her interests confined to music. She clamored for a community center where parents and teachers could work together with the children, and she wrote gently philosophic articles on nature which again remind one of Emerson. And when Emma Jane Jones organized a program for the Grange, people came from all over the County.

The parlor of the house in Emma's day was not the usual musty funeral-biding room. It was always open and often filled with music. In the summer evenings, after the busy day, the hired hands and the smaller children sat outside the open windows to listen to the music from Emma's piano. Someone sang. Robert stood between the windows, tossed his hair out of his eyes, and solemnly played "To a Wild Rose" on his violin. There was an ancient hoptoad who appeared when the music began, to sit throughout the concert on his special rock. The dog and the cats, members of the family, wandered in and out of the house. The small blind mare moved about without a tether, munching grass.

His father had bought Robert his violin when he was nine, and he had lessons from Mr. Gibson who drove over from Henniker each week. When schoolwork and chores were done and his two brothers raced to the river to fish or went off to join a game of baseball at which they both excelled, Robert was allowed, if he chose to, to practice, or sit and draw, or to disappear into the barn cupola to read or dream his interminable dreams.

There were six children in all. The three boys. And then three girls.

The children got their love of reading from their father. While the household raged about him, Fred sat reading, reading. If it disturbed him to have to search for a quiet place in his home, if after his day's work to provide for his family he was dismayed to see pats of butter, a few eggs, vegetables, and fruit pressed upon parting guests by Emma in her compulsive generosity, he gave little sign. He lost himself in Dickens and Scott and Cooper, and he felt no need to share his pleasure in them with anyone. He was a silent man.

In that house, filled with books collected through the generations, there was no censorship of what the children might read. Robert read *The Water Babies* and *Thanatopsis* side by side, and his head rang with poetry as he wandered about the farm even though he sometimes had no notion of what the words meant. He read rapidly and omnifariously as a child and all his life, equally absorbed by Greek architecture, esoteric philosophy, travel, science fiction, and slick paper magazines. Only modern novels failed to interest him. They could not fire his imagination.

He had been given crayons and pencils when he was hardly more than a baby. By the time he was nine he knew he would like to be an artist. He was given instruction in drawing but refused to work at set patterns of cubes and ellipses. Instead he drew airplanes, quantities of wonderful airplanes, when no one in Milton Township had ever seen an airplane. He thought deeply about the pictures he found in his books, and he formed his own idea of what an artist did. "An artist thought of something then he put it down and it stayed."

How then did he come to choose as his own special form the ephemeral art of the theatre? Until he went to Harvard he had not known theatre. He had of course read plays, had even acted in them at school, but in Boston he discovered in the theatres and the vaudeville houses a world of which he'd had no conception. For all his love of music—and he played his violin with the Harvard Pierian Sodality Orchestra—he never visited Boston's Symphony Hall. He waited outside the gallery doors of the theatres to be first for the gallop up the stairs and into the front row, to hang between heaven and earth to hear— he could barely see them from his perch—the great theatre stars. He seldom missed a new act at Keith's vaudeville house, either. He returned to his dormitory to drape sheets over his classmates and to direct them through the lines of SALOMÉ. He enrolled in Professor Baker's course in drama, but Baker overlooked him for the Baker's Dozen, the select group which met with him in his home in the evenings, and Robert, incapable of asking to join, paced the sidewalk outside the Baker house like a rejected swain.

At this time, though his mind was made up to be an artist, he was still thinking in terms of portrait painting. Theatre was sheer pleasure to him, something his puritanical inheritance refused to allow him to think of as a career. When he at last succeeded in combining design and painting with theatre, he was profoundly grateful. In 1915, his career just beginning, he wrote his mother, "Life has become so wonderful to me, beyond words. I have so much work to do I can't possibly do it, all wonderful work, just what I want to do. I wonder how many people have that luxury, of living by the work that makes them happiest and most content? I want you to be glad, because you are going to see me become a real influence on the American theatre."

LEGACY

Rᴏʙᴇʀᴛ Eᴅᴍᴏɴᴅ Jᴏɴᴇs, as an artist and as a person, was a unique combination of craftsman, romantic, mystic, and Puritan. His feeling for the materials he worked with and his skill in manipulating them were akin to those of our colonial craftsmen who gave a clear and enduring beauty to their silverware, chairs and chests, porticos and staircases, their steeples and weather vanes, frigates and figureheads. His profession was less a calling than a call, like the "call" that led some of his New England forebears to the pulpit. The soul to be saved was the theatre's. His aim, throughout his career, was not only to recover its pristine purity and splendor by his own efforts but also to inspire all workers in the theatre—authors, actors, directors, as well as fellow designers—to enlist in his crusade. Almost every one of his lectures and essays collected in *The Dramatic Imagination* is an exhortation. The standards he invokes are not only aesthetic but moral. The scene designer is engaged in a perpetual struggle with sin and salvation—the theatre's and his own. Design that is fundamental will redeem the theatre; every lapse from it will hasten the theatre's eventual doom. Jones's work was not simply a profession, in the accepted sense, but a continual dedication. For he possessed both the vision of an artist and the imagination of a militant visionary.

It was during a single season in Berlin (1913-14) while watching the repertory of Max Reinhardt's *Deutsches Theater* that Jones, who until then, as a young instructor at Harvard, had done little more than paint a few conventional portraits and several effective posters, became aware of the technique of organizing a production then known as "the new stagecraft"—the fusion of acting, lighting, and setting into a dramatic whole. A year later he made his professional début in New York with the sensationally successful setting and costumes for THE MAN WHO MARRIED A DUMB WIFE. Four years later, with THE JEST, he achieved maturity as an artist completely in command of all of the resources of his craft, displaying the unity of style, characteristic of all his later work, that never congealed into a formula.

For the remaining twenty-five years of his active career, every script, whether classic or contemporary, was a fresh stimulus to experiment. His versatility was prodigious—the decorative fantasies and fantastic exaggerations for the ballets TIL EULENSPIEGEL and SKYSCRAPERS; settings for revue sketches at Radio City and its original Roxyettes, for operas and operettas at the renovated goldminers' theatre at Central City, for the naive folk imagery of THE GREEN PASTURES; monumental units for HAMLET and RICHARD III; mordant realism for O'Neill's MOURNING BECOMES ELECTRA and THE ICEMAN COMETH; symbolic abstractions for MACBETH; period decorations for revivals of LOVE FOR LOVE and FASHION; genteel backgrounds for the amiable frivolities of Clare Kummer or the urbanities of S. N. Behrman and Philip Barry. Throughout this theatrical range Jones revealed his outstanding characteristic: his ability to envisage any type of production as a dynamic whole.

This unity, achieved by a director interpreting a script as directly as a conductor interprets a musical score, and expected of any theatrical performance today by both critics and audience, was an innovation less than fifty years old when Jones first witnessed it in Berlin —the evolution of a tradition established by two pioneers, the Duke of Saxe-Meiningen and Adolphe Appia.

The Duke not only directed his repertory company with minute attention to the gestures and movements of every individual in a mob scene; he also designed every setting (he was an accomplished draftsman), supervised its lighting (he was one of the first to use arc lamps in conjunction with gaslight), and selected every bit of material for costumes which he designed to the last detail. He was the first to bring to the European stage the authentic beauty of historic styles at a time when tragedy queens still appeared in a combination of classic draperies and crinolines. From his company's Berlin début in 1874 through their subsequent appearances in all the capitals of Europe—in Paris and Moscow he made converts of Antoine and Stanislavski—the Meiningen productions of JULIUS CAESAR and MACBETH, Schiller's MAID OF ORLEANS and WILLIAM TELL, were sensational revelations of the interpretative power of a new stagecraft.

Appia, in his prophetic book, *Music and Stage Setting* (1899), and in his drawings, foresaw the dramatic importance of stage lighting. Some twenty years before the lighting apparatus by which it could be achieved was even invented, Appia envisioned lighting which would have the direct emotional impact of music, a visual score to accompany the actor; lighting which could define structural forms and, with its fluctuating chiaroscuro, contract the stage to a climactic playing area, or enlarge it to the seemingly infinite spaces of atmospheric horizons.

But to Jones the integration of a performance, however complete and successful, was not the goal. Organization in itself was not enough. As he put it, "... a drama is not an engine, running at full speed from the overture to the final curtain, but *a living organism*" (the italics are mine). What he searched for unremittingly in every script and sought to reveal in every one of his productions was the *élan vital*, the rhythmic throb of life in a living organism, plant, animal, or man. His constant endeavor was to discover the inner rhythm of a play, and then to embody it in the fluctuating emphasis of lighting, in the costuming of the actors, and in the relation of the spaces they moved in to the total composition of his setting—and with that embodiment to achieve the intensification of experience common to all great poetry and painting.

Realism remained the besetting sin. Recalling a performance of HEDDA GABLER, he exclaims, "Here is no solemn public ritual, no spoken opera, but a kind of betrayal. We are all eavesdroppers, peering through a keyhole, minding other people's business." The proscenium arch becomes an enlarged peephole, although it never inhibited Jones to the slightest degree: he successfully ignored it even in his most stylized productions, deliberately used it as an ornamental border for several of his period revivals, made it a symbolic frame for one of his last projects, HENRY VIII. Nevertheless he saw the tentacles of the factual and the photographic reaching out and threatening to establish a stranglehold on the stage. Though he paid a passing tribute to O'Neill—(his work "would be outstanding in any period of theatre history")—he believed that "in the main the dramas of our time are as literal as if they had been dictated by the village iceman or a parlor-maid peering through a keyhole." Too many contemporary playwrights seem engaged in "a kind of tacit conspiracy . . . to rob the theatre of its ancient mystery and its ancient awe."

Jones's feeling for the theatre was fundamentally romantic. "Romance and glamour have always seemed to me to be the very foundation of the theatre. . . . I believe that audiences naturally crave a theatre of poetry and mystery and magic. . . . Every play is a living dream: your dream, my dream. . . . Every heroine is the princess in the fairy-tale and every hero is a hero of romance. The characters on the stage are really Olympian beings. . . . They are themselves glamour." Stage lighting must "bathe our productions in the light that never was on sea or land." In lighting a stage, "animating the scene moment by moment until it seems to breathe, our work becomes an incantation. We feel in the presence of elemental energies."

Though the language is rhapsodic, these assertions are not the credo of an aspiring spirit beating its wings ineffectually in a void. While planning a production Jones was as deliberately and shrewdly practical as a Yankee farmer pruning fruit trees or fertilizing a field before planting a crop. In designing his costumes, for instance, he assembled swatches of every bit of material to be used, often pinning or basting costumes together for the dressmaker, or, if the need arose as it did in Caliban, completing an array of hundreds of costumes with the aid of only a few assistants. He conscientiously absorbed source material, traveling to England to study the Tower of London at first hand for Richard III, spending several months in Venice before starting his first Othello, poring over the original Chinese documents of Lute Song. But these were mere preliminaries to the process of creation, or rather re-creation—the process of interpreting, intensifying, and re-fashioning every characteristic detail of architecture, the line and sweep of every costume, its encrustations and ornaments, until he achieved a vibrant pattern of light, texture, and form that sustained the play's dominant mood, heightened its pattern of emotions, and illuminated its inner meaning. As he stated it, "The energy of a particular play, its emotional content, its aura, so to speak, has its own definite physical dimensions. . . . In the last analysis the designing of stage scenery is not the problem of an architect or a painter or a sculptor or even of a musician, but of a poet." The theatre that Jones with unflagging energy labored to create was a theatre where designers worked with playwrights who were dramatic poets, and where a new race of actors would perfect "an art of musical speaking that is almost unknown in our day. When a playwright begins to awaken the music that lies in the spoken word, and when an actor begins to give this music its value, a new theatre springs into being"—a theatre that achieves the compassionate purgation of tragedy and the no less compassionate insight of high comedy.

"Out of the manifold contacts of my experience the image of a new theatre has gradually formed itself—a theatre not yet made with hands. I look forward to this ideal theatre and work toward it."

This image was part of the threefold legacy that Jones bequeathed to the theatre. He was the first to win recognition in this country for the scenic designer as an indispensable collaborator in the interpretation of a script. His life, as well as his credo, is an enduring stimulus not only to his contemporaries but to their successors. His drawings, unlike so many designs for the theatre, express the total beauty and impact of his productions as performed and help them to remain living memories. As I once expressed it in a sonnet,

>   . . . Here the alloy
> Of Thought and Passion, blurred in our separate days,
> Became a silver mirror, wherein Joy
> Could pierce to Sorrow's wisdom; in the ways
> Of Fate, trod by the footsteps of a mime,
> We could meet Death but triumph over Time.

PRACTICAL DREAMS

Robert Edmond Jones could be described as a dreamer, but he was also a doer. Idealist he was, but certainly he cannot be dismissed as a mere visionary. A prophet, yes, but at the same time a most practical craftsman. When Bobby decided on an effect he wanted to achieve for the ghost in Hamlet, he was not content to record his conception of the scene in a painting, however beautiful it might be; he had to sit down with his master electrician, George Schaff, show him the painting, and interpret it for him in terms of the ideas which were emerging from the creative depths of his own imagination. For Jones was fortunate in having in George Schaff a fellow artist as well as a fine craftsman, and Jones knew how fortunate he was. He relied, of course, on Schaff's technical assurance and sensitive understanding; but also he insisted on sharing with George Schaff the stimulation of his own personal fire.

When I worked as Jones's apprentice, I used to sit in on these meetings in Bobby's studio on 39th Street. They were not the conversations one would normally expect between an electrician and a scene designer. For hours on end, as one would talk with a playwright or a stage director, Jones would discuss with Schaff all the subtleties of sensitive light changes from the beginning to the end of the play; and when words proved inadequate, Bobby's mood drawings would illustrate and clarify the difficult points. At these meetings there would be no reference to specific pieces of equipment or to the numbers of gelatin colors —not that Jones wasn't perfectly familiar with them, but that he was dealing with his master electrician in his own way. Finally he would say, "George, when you're ready to show me the scene, call me." And then, sometime in the early hours of the morning, I would get a call from Schaff at the theatre: "Tell Bobby to come on over, I've got something to show him."

As he came backstage, Bobby always insisted on closing his eyes to avoid seeing the stage picture from the wings. Slowly he'd grope his way out to the rear of the darkened auditorium, and then for the first time he would look at the magic they had planned together. If the result was not completely satisfactory, more discussion, more experimentation would follow; for no night was too long, no dawn too cold to keep Bobby from sitting there hour after hour until the lights were right.

Union working rules ultimately became so limiting that the artist's "efficiency" in the organization of his ideas, and his ability to carry them out in minimum time, took on an import almost equal to his creative talent. But Bobby Jones and George Schaff, an ideal collaboration between the creative artist and the artist-craftsman, were, in this case, fortunate enough to work together in a day when the clock and the calendar played relatively minor roles in the creative process. Later, when Bobby no longer had the services of George Schaff, he would sit down with Eddie Kook and tell *him* about the wonders he imagined for what was to happen on the stage. And, of course, he constantly made wonderful drawings.

Jones's drawings were essentially means to an *end*. His inspiration was always firmly rooted in the demands and limitations of the living theatre. Gordon Craig, even Adolphe Appia at times, created many evocative designs intended solely to express an ideal. Were they to be executed faithfully by loyal disciples, most of them would dwarf the living actor and spill out beyond the physical limits of the tallest proscenium and the deepest stage. When Jones *wrote* about the theatre, he was constantly endeavoring, like Craig and Appia, to clarify our vision of what the theatre can be at its highest level of achievement. But when he *designed* for the theatre, he worked strictly within the technical resources of the theatre immediately available to him, the American theatre of the first half of the twentieth century. When his projects—some of them, like THE CENCI, so highly imaginative—were unproduced, it was never for reasons of technical limitations in the designs themselves. Much as he loved to paint and draw—and Bobby would chortle with glee when finishing a particularly beautiful painting—his pleasure was only partly derived from the creation of the moment; much more important was his clear perception of what this design could become *in the theatre*.

I recall the time when Jones was supervising the execution of the stage setting for the seventeenth-century Spanish room in THE BUCCANEER. A week earlier he had completed his design, and on this particular day the crew of fine scenic artists in Bergman's Studio was executing the set on the paint-frame below Jones's studio. Bobby couldn't bear the idea that they would think of their work as simply the job of executing a large painting; so he scurried out with me to gather up bits and pieces of what he called "living things" which related to the setting: a lovely antique bench of the period with the patina of age and the beauty of line that he loved so much; a swatch of antique yellow satin, with some black lace and a huge artifical red flower; a yard or two of heavy gold lace; one lovely Spanish Renaissance tile. These things he placed on the floor beside the setting on which the painters were at work, because Jones wanted—for himself and for all who were working with him—to be conscious of the relations of this painting to its final achievement and appearance on the stage.

Early in his career Jones was disappointed to find that his first reproduced designs had lost so many of their values, no matter how carefully the photographer and the engraver had done their work. Bobby promptly set to work to discover what had to be done to compensate for this loss. Every time he did a new play, he made drawings with this problem in mind until he had mastered a technique usually understood only by professional illustrators who deal every day with these problems of reproduction. With extreme practicality this dreamer saw to it that the record of his work could be reproduced with vitality and beauty, and his grasp of the techniques involved was so sure that he could explain them to me in full and careful detail on a day when I was trying to cope with a similar disappointment at seeing a reproduction of one of my own designs.

Jones was never content to enjoy the beauty of his magnificent costume designs as pure painting—or even, with swatches of fabrics and lace and braids pinned to the sketch, as indications of what a costume was going to be. His costumes were meant, not just for an audience to look at, but for actors to *act* in. As he wrote in one of his early essays, "Costuming is not dressmaking. It is a matter of understanding the dramatist's inner idea, of knowing how the actors carry out this intention in their movements and of arranging drapery to make these movements seem more expressive and more heroic. The problem of costume is the problem of the man who wears it and of what he is trying to do and say in it."

One morning Bobby told me to report early to the Eaves costume workshop instead of to the studio as was usual. When I arrived, I was told to go to Fitting Room A. I knocked. I opened the door. There in front of me was the back of a seventeenth-century lady bent over in a deep and exaggerated curtsy. Her wig was rich with trimming, and the hand that held her train was loaded with period jewelry and roped with pearls. I glanced beyond this magnificent figure into the mirror. There, between the baroque pearl necklace and the rich hairdressing was Bobby Jones's eager face—black brows, piercing eyes looking through his glasses, and a broad grin under the clipped black mustache. He laughed. "You know, Jo," he said, "most actresses really don't know how to wear these things. I just had to see what it felt like." He moved about the room in the splendid gown. "It's wonderful, don't you think?" This little performance was typical of Jones's attitude toward anything in the theatre, whether it was designing a small hand prop or a full setting or even the tiny buckle of a period shoe. Never was he interested in a stage picture for the picture's sake alone. Everything had to be related to the play so that the play might achieve its stature as living theatre.

Very early in Jones's career he became conscious of what a powerful medium stage lighting is for the theatre artist. From the early 1920's on, Jones never developed a design without constant consideration of what light would do to form and to color. Shadow was no longer for him just the absence of light, but in itself something to be mastered and controlled and made expressive. From the time he started the great series of productions for Arthur Hopkins (in contrast to his earlier designs from THE MAN WHO MARRIED A DUMB WIFE up to the Hopkins production of HEDDA GABLER), the brilliance, the imaginative scope of Jones's designs, were enormously heightened by his sensitive control of the power and beauty of dramatic lighting.

There was never a detail of lighting, setting, costumes, or properties that Bobby didn't want to supervise personally and with the most minute attention; he always resented the slowly increasing need for help. Even in the early 1920's, after such achievements as TIL EULENSPIEGEL and REDEMPTION and RICHARD III, he was still making his own working drawings for the carpenter or the prop maker. Although intended for no one's eyes but the craftsman's concerned, these shop drawings were in themselves works of art. Usually made on a good grade of brown drafting paper, they were often enhanced by added touches with a red pencil, or a blue with a black. Sometimes a quote from the play or a line from a poem was tastefully written in Jones's strong and vivid handwriting in just the right spot on the page. If Bobby were asked, "Do you think Adam Tait, the carpenter, will really understand it?" he probably would laugh and say, "Perhaps he won't." And then with a serious look in his eye he would add, "Perhaps he will."

As the pressures of his professional work increased, I urged Bobby to let me make these shop drawings on tracing paper and have them blueprinted. He was shocked at the idea, horrified that mechanical reproduction would rob his drawings of the personal touch which he always loved. (Eventually—and most reluctantly—Bobby gave in.)

This passion for reaching for the highest in every detail of his work is also illustrated by his attitude toward the actors in productions which he designed. I recall that Arthur Hopkins' business manager very hesitantly and politely inquired of Bobby one day, "Is it necessary to have those eighteenth-century quills and sand shakers on the desk upstage in the corner of the set? You must realize, Mr. Jones, that even the first row of the orchestra can't appreciate an object so small at that distance." Bobby turned and glared. "Do you think," he said, "that only people on the other side of the footlights need exaltation? What about the actor? Surely he should *feel* the *sense of period* when working in this set!"

Another example of Bobby's desire to stimulate the actors' imaginations was his conversation with them at their first costume fittings— long before satin and laces were ready to take the place of muslin and pins. Each actor was shown the beautiful drawing for his costume, and then Bobby discussed with him the problems of movement and attitude and style imposed by the modes and manners of the period. He was quick to resent indifference, but he was wonderfully appreciative and loyal to those who found—as most actors did—that Bobby's sincerity and thoroughness as a craftsman provided a challenging stimulant to the further development of their roles. Even among those who might not be sensitive enough to appreciate the deeper qualities of his creativity, Bobby's complete artistic integrity won him countless friends in the theatre.

In matters of taste, in the conduct of his personal life, Bobby Jones could easily retreat into the fastidious perfections of his ivory tower and enjoy its remoteness from the outside world; but as a working artist he was never *précieux*. He was that rare admixture—an enormously creative artist whose dreams came true on the stage.

PLATES

The fifty-one plates which follow have all been made for this volume from the original designs of Robert Edmond Jones, through the courtesy of their various owners. Each caption provides the basic facts which identify the design; further details concerning the production or project are available in the Chronology, which begins on page 144.

Jones frequently worked in black and white; he used color in less than half of the drawings reproduced here. Eight of these plates are the actual size of the originals and are so indicated. The others have been reduced from drawings of various dimensions. Most of these reductions have been relatively slight, although in a few instances — notably Skyscrapers and Yolanda of Cyprus — the reproductions are less than half the size of the originals.

At the time of his death, Jones was in process of selecting designs for a new volume of drawings which he hoped to publish; thirty-eight of the plates in the present volume are from designs included in the various lists he compiled.

1913
Percy Bysshe Shelley: THE CENCI
Act V, Scene IV — *The Hall of the Prison*
Project for Arena Staging
Courtesy of Mr. Jo Mielziner

1915

Anatole France: THE MAN WHO MARRIED A DUMB WIFE
Before the House of Judge Leonard Botal in Paris
For Harley Granville-Barker
This is the original design for the setting of
Jones's first professional assignment. In actual
production and in later drawings based on the pro-
duction he altered the design considerably.
Courtesy of Margaret Hewes

1918

Leo Tolstoi: REDEMPTION
Preliminary Sketch for Act I, Scene II —
The House of the Gypsies
(Actual Size)
For Arthur Hopkins
Courtesy of Mrs. William E. Pennington

1920

John Alden Carpenter: THE BIRTHDAY OF THE INFANTA
Scene II — *The Hall of the Mirrors*
For the Chicago Opera Association
Courtesy of Mr. Lee Simonson

1920

William Shakespeare: KING RICHARD III
Act I, Scene II — *The Wooing of Lady Anne*
(Actual Size)
For Arthur Hopkins
Courtesy of Mr. Lee Simonson

1921

William Shakespeare: MACBETH
Act III, Scene IV — *The Banquet Scene*
For Arthur Hopkins
Courtesy of Mrs. Honor Leeming Luttgen

1921

William Shakespeare: MACBETH
Act V, Scene I — *The Sleepwalking Scene*
(Actual Size)
For Arthur Hopkins
Courtesy of Mrs. Honor Leeming Luttgen

1921

Sidney Howard: SWORDS
A Castle in Calabria
(Actual Size)
For Brock Pemberton
Courtesy of the Enthoven Theatre Collection,
Victoria and Albert Museum

c. 1921

Maurice Maeterlinck — Claude Debussy:
Pelléas et Mélisande
Act IV, Scene III — *The Fountain*
Project
Courtesy of Mrs. Frances G. Wickes

1922

William Shakespeare: HAMLET
Act IV, Scene V — *The Madness of Ophelia*
For Arthur Hopkins
Courtesy of Mr. Lee Simonson

1922

William Shakespeare: HAMLET
Act V, Scene I — *The Burial of Ophelia*
For Arthur Hopkins
Courtesy of Mrs. William E. Pennington

c. 1923

Melchior Lengyel: THE KINGDOM OF SANCHO PANZA
Design for Peasant Costume
Project
Courtesy of Mr. Jo Mielziner

1924

Luigi Pirandello: AT THE GATEWAY
A Cemetery
For Maria Carmi
Courtesy of the Theatre Collection,
Museum of the City of New York

52

1924
Eugene O'Neill: DESIRE UNDER THE ELMS
The Cabot Homestead
(Actual Size)
For Experimental Theatre, Inc.
Courtesy of Mrs. Walter Huston

1925
Eugene O'Neill: THE FOUNTAIN
Part II, Scene V — *The Torture of Nano*
For Macgowan, Jones, and O'Neill
Courtesy of Mrs. William E. Pennington

56

1925
William Shakespeare: MUCH ADO ABOUT NOTHING
Act II, Scene I — *Masquerade Costume for Hero*
For the Theatre Guild, Inc. Not produced.
Courtesy of Mrs. Mary Hall Furber

HERO
(Masquerade)

Sash of soft
powder-blue.

1926

John Alden Carpenter: SKYSCRAPERS
Scene VI — *Steel Girders*
For the Metropolitan Opera Association
Courtesy of Mr. Benjamin L. Webster

1927

Louis Bromfield: THE HOUSE OF WOMEN
The Parlor of the Shane House
(Actual Size)
For Arthur Hopkins
Courtesy of Mr. John Mason Brown

62

1927
Gabriele D'Annunzio: LA GIOCONDA
Act III — *The Anteroom of the Sculptor's Studio*
Project
Courtesy of Mrs. Frances G. Wickes

1928

Charles Gounod: Fᴀᴜsᴛ
Act III — *A Public Square: Mephisto's Serenade*
For the American Opera Company
Courtesy of the Adams Memorial Theatre,
Williams College

1928

Sophie Treadwell: MACHINAL
Episode VIII — *Courtroom*
(Actual Size)
For Arthur Hopkins
Courtesy of Mrs. William E. Pennington

1929

Cale Young Rice — Clarence Loomis:
YOLANDA OF CYPRUS
Act III — *The Council Chamber*
For the American Opera Company
Courtesy of Mr. Raymond Sovey

70

1930
Marc Connelly: THE GREEN PASTURES
Illustration for Part I, Scene VIII —
The Lord Shows Noah His Plan for Building the Ark
For Farrar and Rinehart, Inc.
Courtesy of Mrs. Frances G. Wickes

1930
Marc Connelly: THE GREEN PASTURES
Illustration for Part II, Scene IV —
The Prayer of Moses
For Farrar and Rinehart, Inc.
Courtesy of Mrs. Frances G. Wickes

74

1930
Marc Connelly: THE GREEN PASTURES
Illustration for Part II, Scene VII —
The Vision of Hezdrel
For Farrar and Rinehart, Inc.
Courtesy of Mrs. Frances G. Wickes

1930

Arturo Rossato — Felice Lattuada: LE PREZIOSE RIDICOLE
Founded on Molière's LES PRÉCIEUSES RIDICULES
Preliminary Sketch for Proscenium and Front Curtain
For the Metropolitan Opera Association
Courtesy of Mr. Jo Mielziner

1931

Jean Cocteau — Igor Stravinsky: OEDIPUS REX
Preliminary Sketch
For the League of Composers in association with
Leopold Stokowski and the Philadelphia Orchestra
Courtesy of Mrs. Arthur M. Reis

1931

Eugene O'Neill: MOURNING BECOMES ELECTRA
Exterior of the Mannon House
(Actual Size)
For the Theatre Guild, Inc.
Courtesy of the Theatre Collection,
Museum of the City of New York

82

1932

Maxwell Anderson: NIGHT OVER TAOS
The Great Hall of the Montoya Hacienda
For the Group Theatre, Inc.
Courtesy of Mr. and Mrs. Irving Schwartzkopf

1932
Alexandre Dumas, fils: CAMILLE
Act III — *Auteuil*
For the Central City Opera House Association
Courtesy of Mrs. Delos Chappell

1932
Alexandre Dumas, fils: CAMILLE
Act V — *Marguerite's Bedroom*
For the Central City Opera House Association
Courtesy of Miss Lillian Gish

1937
William Shakespeare: OTHELLO
Act II, Scene III —
The Duel between Cassio and Roderigo
For Max Gordon
Courtesy of the Museum of Modern Art

90

1937
William Shakespeare: OTHELLO
Act V, Scene II — *A Bedchamber*
For Max Gordon
Courtesy of the Museum of Modern Art

1939
Philip Barry: THE PHILADELPHIA STORY
Act II —
The Porch of Seth Lord's House in the Country
For the Theatre Guild, Inc.
Courtesy of Miss Katharine Hepburn

c. 1940
Maurice Maeterlinck: PELLÉAS ET MÉLISANDE
A Corridor in the Castle
Project for a Marionette Production
Courtesy of Mrs. Mary Hall Furber

1941

Gioacchino Rossini: THE BARBER OF SEVILLE
Prologue
For the Central City Opera House Association
Courtesy of the Central City Opera House Association

1941
William Shakespeare: KING RICHARD III
Act I, Scene I — *The Vision of the Crown*
Project for a Unit Setting with Projected Effects
Courtesy of the Adams Memorial Theatre,
Williams College

1941

William Shakespeare: KING RICHARD III
Act V, Scene III — *The Ghost of Lady Anne*
Project for a Unit Setting with Projected Effects
Courtesy of Dr. and Mrs. Councilman Morgan

1942
Paul Vincent Carroll: THE OLD FOOLISHNESS
Act II — *A Ruined Castle in Ireland*
Project
Courtesy of Dr. Bertram Schaffner

104

1942

THE LORDS OF THE WEST (author unknown)
Act III — *A Battlemented Fortress*
Project
Courtesy of Mr. and Mrs. Robert Popper

1944
William Shakespeare: KING HENRY VIII
Act II, Scene I — *Buckingham's Farewell*
For Billy Rose. Not produced.
Courtesy of the Jones Estate

1944
William Shakespeare: KING HENRY VIII
Act II, Scene IV —
Blackfriars: The Trial of Queen Katherine
For Billy Rose. Not produced.
Courtesy of the Jones Estate

110

1944
William Shakespeare: King Henry VIII
Act III, Scene I — *The Queen's Apartment*
For Billy Rose. Not produced.
Courtesy of the Jones Estate

112

1944
William Shakespeare: KING HENRY VIII
Act IV, Scene I — *The Coronation*
For Billy Rose. Not produced.
Courtesy of the Jones Estate

1946

Sidney Howard and Will Irwin: LUTE SONG
A Curtain
For Michael Myerberg
Courtesy of Mr. Arthur P. Segal

1946
Sidney Howard and Will Irwin: Lute Song
Act II, Scene V — *The Street of Shops*
For Michael Myerberg
Courtesy of the Museum of Modern Art

1946
Sidney Howard and Will Irwin: LUTE SONG
Act III, Scene VI —
The Blue Pavilion in the Palace of Prince Nieou
For Michael Myerberg
Courtesy of the Museum of Modern Art

120

1946

Eugene O'Neill: THE ICEMAN COMETH
The Back Room and a Section of the Bar at Harry Hope's
For the Theatre Guild, Inc.
Courtesy of the University of Minnesota Theatre

1946
Eugene O'Neill: A Touch of the Poet
Dining Room of Melody's Tavern
Project
Courtesy of the Jones Estate

1946

William Shakespeare: MACBETH
Act V, Scene I — *The Sleepwalking Scene*
Project
Courtesy of the Jones Estate

126

[Date uncertain]

William Shakespeare: MACBETH
Act V, Scene I — *The Sleepwalking Scene*
For Jane Cowl. Not produced.
Courtesy of Mr. Donald M. Oenslager

128

"SETTINGS BY ROBERT EDMOND JONES"

IT HAS BEEN said that a man who works with his hands is a workman; a man who works with his hands and his head is a craftsman; and when that man also works with his heart, he is an artist. Since his first production, THE MAN WHO MARRIED A DUMB WIFE, Robert Edmond Jones always combined these three roles with triple felicity.

After his *Wanderjahr* in Europe, Jones returned to the New York scene to assault the theatre's stronghold of false realism. As an artist, fortified with his vision of "the new stagecraft," he opened new doors and illuminated new paths, and as a craftsman, he discovered new ways and means of employing canvas and scene-paint and light. His designs were never embroidered with realism but suggested mood by understatement and revealed the essence of a scene with dramatic imagination. In his Foreword to *Drawings for the Theatre* he was the artist thinking of his craft as he wrote, "The scene designer is forced to work and think in a hundred different ways—now as an architect, now as a house-painter, now as an electrician, now as a dressmaker, now as a sculptor, now as a jeweler. He must make idols and palaces and necklaces and frescoes and caparisons. As he works, he may be all too well aware of the outward limitations of the play he is to decorate and the actors he is to clothe. But in his mind's eye he must see the high original intention of the dramatist and follow it." For him the scene designer was a man of many minds. According to the dictates of the drama, he thought in terms of realism or surrealism, of impressionism or expres-

LUTE SONG: Design for Act III, Scene VI—
The Blue Pavilion in the Palace of Prince
Nieou. (A larger reproduction of this design
appears as a plate facing page 120.)

sionism, or symbolism. He trained his eye on the conventions of all the arts, past and present. Yet while he was a man of many minds, every production was invariably finished with the patina of his own special polish.

Working as an apprentice to Mr. Jones on the costumes for PATIENCE at the Provincetown Theatre, I recall how deftly and surely his mind worked. On stationery from the old Lafayette Hotel, where he lived, he talked with his pencil about Bunthorne and about his accessories which I was to find. "Here, let me show you—this is what I mean! *Here* he is." And with a few incisive velvet-black pencil strokes, he dramatized aesthetic Bunthorne all in black with sunflower, pheasant quill, perfume vial, and vellum notebook on a gilt chain—all there larger than life—because as a craftsman he knew exactly how he wanted Bunthorne the actor to look on the stage. With Jones, the actors and their costumes came first; then he designed the setting around them.

Working on a sketch for a setting is probably the happiest and briefest part of the artist's work in the theatre. Jones had the gift of embodying his fully developed idea for a scene within his first chiaroscuro sketch, and it was extraordinary how invariably right that scene was for the play. The craft of translating this sketch and resolving it into a full-scale, three-dimensional setting on the stage consumes most of the designer's time. He becomes a service institution, providing ground plans, scale drawings, and hanging plot for the builder, painter's elevations for the scenic studio, costume sketches, and light plot. His studio is an information center for all those workers concerned with the visual aspects of a production.

For many years Jones's studio was a dusty gray room, a kind of never-never land, up three rickety flights of open stairs suspended high above the spattered paint bridge of Robert W. Bergman's Scenic Studio on West 39th Street. Through dim windows loomed the iron fire escapes clinging to the forlorn brick walls of the Metropolitan Opera House across the street. From this murky studio came many of his most brilliant productions. That was his service station, and heavenward, to see Mr. Jones, climbed a constant procession of producers, directors, and all the theatre's craftsmen: builders, scenic artists, electricians, property men, costumers, upholsterers, and flower makers. When he was engaged on a production, there was always quiet confusion in his studio. Then suddenly, "I can't take it any more," and Jones would retreat down the stairs and dash out to a Broadway theatre for a light rehearsal, a scene rehearsal, a dress rehearsal, or more often to become lost in the catacombs of New York on some unholy mission spotting properties—China Export tea cups, a patchwork quilt, a Byzantine crucifix, a fragment of baroque carving. These diverse activities constituted general supervision, and were standard procedure for every production he designed.

Jones's designs for Lute Song were perhaps his last significant and most admired work. The play was presented by Michael Myerberg in February 1946, at the Plymouth Theatre, where Jones had created settings and costumes for so many notable productions in collaboration with Arthur Hopkins.

Sidney Howard and Will Irwin had adapted Lute Song from the popular Chinese classic drama, Pi-Pa-Ki, a poetic folk play of filial piety and devotion written at the end of the Yuan Dynasty some five

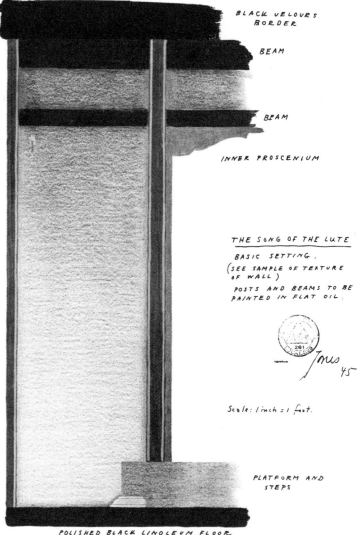

BLACK VELOURS BORDER

BEAM

BEAM

INNER PROSCENIUM

THE SONG OF THE LUTE

BASIC SETTING.
(SEE SAMPLE OF TEXTURE OF WALL)
POSTS AND BEAMS TO BE PAINTED IN FLAT OIL.

Jones
45

Scale: 1 inch = 1 foot.

PLATFORM AND STEPS

POLISHED BLACK LINOLEUM FLOOR

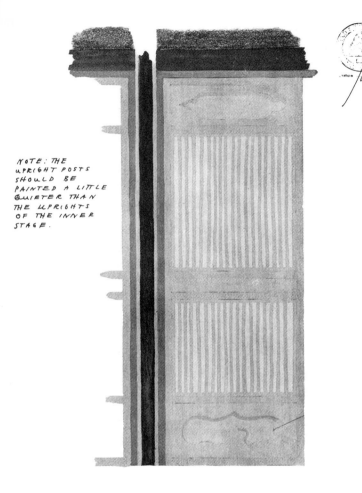

NOTE: THE
UPRIGHT POSTS
SHOULD BE
PAINTED A LITTLE
QUIETER THAN
THE UPRIGHTS
OF THE INNER
STAGE.

THE SONG OF THE LUTE

DETAIL OF SCREEN.
(THE BLUE PAVILLION)

hundred years ago. For fifteen years Lute Song had tempted many producers. It required many scenes varying from complete simplicity to overpowering extravagance. Mr. Myerberg was adventurous, and finally surrendering to the charm of the play, he became so profligate in his plans that the production turned into a major conspiracy of Broadway talent.

Jones worked fourteen months designing the many scenes and hundreds of costumes for the play. Unless under great pressure, he always preferred to make his own working drawings and sketches for properties and costumes accompanied by his inimitable notes for fashioning them, often with illustrations and fabric samples attached. His working drawings are impeccable models of lucid definition and explanation. His blueprint for the Rain Curtain specifies that it be "made of 4-inch strips of shiny satin in several shades of gray brushed with black and silver—should be doubled and stitched at both sides but not lined." He was punctilious regarding details of costumes and accessories. His sketch for the two omnipresent "invisible" Property Men is filled with characteristic notations to guide the costume maker. Before beginning to design, he would gather together from theatrical emporiums many samples of cheap metallic and shiny cloth, tinsel, burlap, printed cottons, and from bargain basements, swatches of theatrical and stagy materials. From this collection emerged his costume sketches for characters from beggars to princes.

With Jones, the craftsman never took over where the artist left off because with him the artist never left off; the felicity and completeness of his drawings were an inspiration to the craftsmen concerned with executing the production. His working drawing for the maker of the great gold Buddha was rendered with such fluency of line that the papier-mâché Buddha on stage seemed wrought by Jones, himself, in the tradition of an Eastern wood carver. This capacity for translating the actual into the exaggerated terms of the theatrical was most characteristic of Jones's work in the theatre.

On the architectural stage of the Chinese theatre, Pi-Pa-Ki would

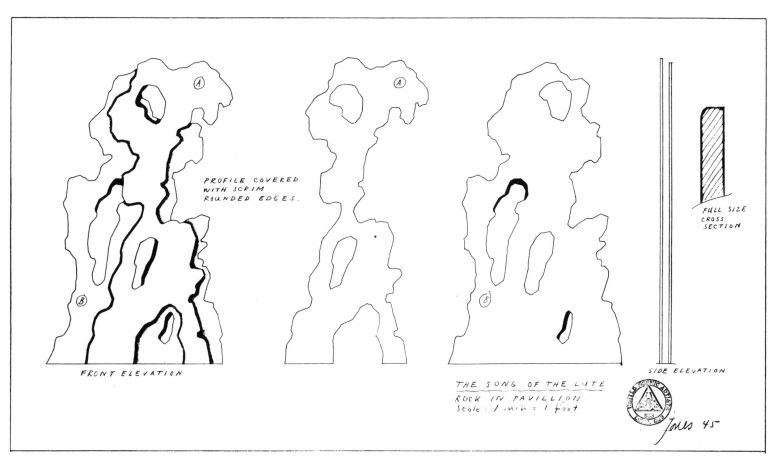

Within the drawing:

PROFILE COVERED
WITH SCRIM
ROUNDED EDGES.

FULL SIZE
CROSS
SECTION

FRONT ELEVATION

THE SONG OF THE LUTE
ROCK IN PAVILLION
Scale: 1 inch = 1 foot

SIDE ELEVATION

Jones 45

LUTE SONG: Act III, Scene VI—
Working drawing for the Garden Stone
in the *Blue Pavilion* of
Prince Nieou.

proceed with only changes of conventional properties, which, as Will Irwin observed, "are never realistic but are always elaborated and heightened to fantastic abstractions of themselves." In designing LUTE SONG's sixteen scenes for our Western stage, Jones's central intention was to achieve in an Oriental story-telling fashion a progression of impressionistic scenes. He devised a neutral basic setting with an inner proscenium to frame accessories that should suggest the many scenes

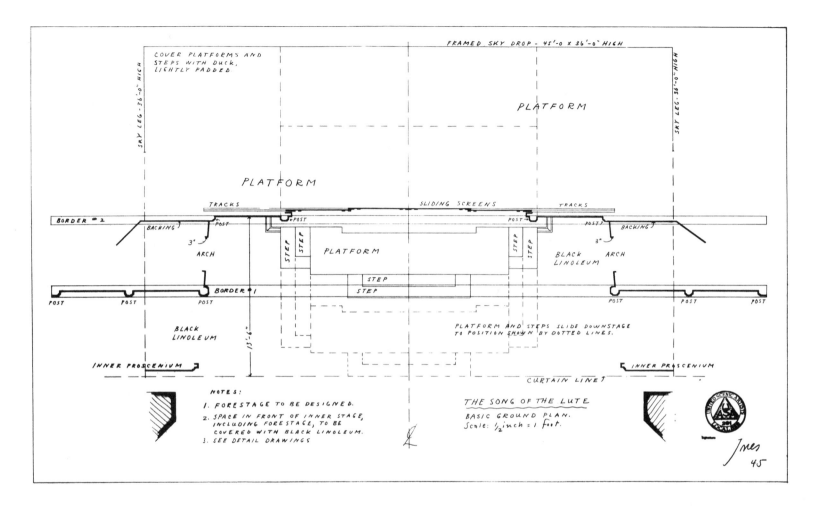

COVER PLATFORMS AND
STEPS WITH DUCK,
LIGHTLY PADDED.

FRAMED SKY DROP - 45'-0 X 36'-0" HIGH

SKY LEG - 36'-0" HIGH

PLATFORM

PLATFORM

SKY LEG - 36'-0" HIGH

BORDER # 2

TRACKS

SLIDING SCREENS

TRACKS

BACKING

POST

POST

POST

POST

BACKING

3"

ARCH

STEP

STEP

PLATFORM

STEP

STEP

BLACK
LINOLEUM

3"

ARCH

STEP

POST

POST

POST

BORDER # 1

STEP

POST

POST

POST

BLACK
LINOLEUM

13'-6"

PLATFORM AND STEPS SLIDE DOWNSTAGE
TO POSITION SHOWN BY DOTTED LINES.

INNER PROSCENIUM

INNER PROSCENIUM

CURTAIN LINE

NOTES:

1. FORESTAGE TO BE DESIGNED.
2. SPACE IN FRONT OF INNER STAGE,
   INCLUDING FORESTAGE, TO BE
   COVERED WITH BLACK LINOLEUM.
3. SEE DETAIL DRAWINGS

THE SONG OF THE LUTE
BASIC GROUND PLAN.
Scale: ½ inch = 1 foot.

Jones
45

which were changed behind transitional sliding screens and parallel
curtains. The formal curtains were suspended on poles by cloud motifs
attached to black velour strips bound with shiny black satin. The scenic
artist's sketch for the basic set was typically Jones, executed in crayon
and gouache on a water-color wash to differentiate the varying surface
textures of grays and blacks.

136 : DONALD OENSLAGER

The inner scenes—a palace, temple, or garden—seemed just right because they no more than suggested the idea of a place, like a passing thought. For the *Blue Pavilion of Prince Nieou,* the inner proscenium framed two grilled screens of soft cobalt and jade. Between them the double profile of a monumental garden stone, also of cobalt, was the Pavilion's only embellishment. Five hundred years ago Jones might have been court designer to Prince Nieou, responsible for devising this Blue Pavilion in addition to fireworks and fountains, festival arrangements, and frequent court entertainments. For LUTE SONG this garden stone serves as his symbol of a Chinese scene, and it would surely have appealed to Prince Nieou. Jones always planned and lighted a scene carefully to enhance the characteristic qualities of actors and their performances. For this scene he dressed the actors in splendid costumes of blue, scarlet, green, and gold, and like an old Yuan painting, the scene of the Blue Pavilion did not really come to life for Jones without the actors playing in light.

Light, with Jones, was a marvelously sensitive medium of expression—so sympathetic that "the livingness of light" for him was almost a sixth sense in the theatre. He thought of lighting as a craft and had

LUTE SONG: Costume sketch for the two Property Men. The notations for the guidance of the costume maker are characteristic of Jones's punctilious attention to detail.

LUTE SONG: Act III, Scene IV—*The Temple of Amidha.* Details from the working drawing for the gold buddha.

LUTE SONG in performance, showing the buddha and the *Blue Pavilion* scene, with Mary Martin as *Tchao-Ou-Niang, the Wife* and Yul Brynner as *Tsai-Yong, the Husband*.

no rules for its use. "Our real problem in the theatre is to know where to put the light and where to take it away." In LUTE SONG he played light like a graded wash over some scenes; at other times, a stabbing spotlight revealed the inner content of a dramatic moment. Scene by scene his use of arbitrary and changing intensities of light activated the forward movement of the drama.

By his rare knowledge of the arts of the East and the theatre conventions of the West, Jones brought notable visual beauty to this old Eastern folk play on Broadway. Alan Priest, Curator of Far Eastern Art in the Metropolitan Museum, with his caring eye, observed that "Mr. Jones's sets melt scene into scene with the movement of an unrolling Chinese scroll, and it is the most beautiful and most true visual interpretation of China that has ever appeared on the Western stage. These sets and the whole presentation would delight the Chinese in China, could it be presented there—the Chinese would understand and like this production from beginning to end."

Robert Edmond Jones was a remarkably perceptive artist and an unerring craftsman. He used his hands, his head, and his heart with imagination and discernment. He could evoke settings on our stage that mirrored his poignant insight into the meaning of all things theatrical. Our theatre is far richer for the spell he cast upon it and for the stature he bequeathed to it.

Of the illustrations appearing in this chapter, the set design, painter's elevations, and costume sketch are reproduced through the courtesy of the Museum of Modern Art; the working drawings, courtesy of the Jones Estate; the photograph at left, above, by George Karger, courtesy of Pix, Inc., and the one below courtesy of Michael Myerberg.

KENNETH MACGOWAN

JONES AS DIRECTOR AND FILM DESIGNER

PRODUCERS AND DIRECTORS who worked with Robert Edmond Jones for the first time were often surprised at the smooth and quick perfection with which he lit the show. Nothing was hurried, nothing frantic. There were no emergencies, no last-minute calls for extra equipment. His lighting plan worked out perfectly. If the director suddenly changed his mind about the atmosphere of a scene, Jones changed his lighting almost as quickly—and let the director discover for himself whether he had made a mistake. The quiet efficiency of the designer on-stage was as remarkable as the restrained but potent quality of his designs.

Why should all this have surprised producers who had never before hired Jones to design a show, and directors who had never worked with him? It was not because the light rehearsals of other scenic artists had seemed a bit more strenuous; for some of them had worked with almost the speed and smoothness of Jones. Men who had never seen him light a show were astonished at this quiet efficiency merely because it was such a contrast to some of the outward qualities of the man they thought they knew. It is hard to describe Jones's personality—especially for one who knew him as I did from his Harvard days, and through three years of close association in production. But I am sure that most men who had never seen him at work upon the stage felt that here was a fellow just a bit too sensitive, too nervously eager, too fired by what seemed to them esoteric theories. A very few

—like Arthur Hopkins, who appeared outwardly so calm, even commonplace—understood Jones's temperament and listened with respect when Jones hinted at such ideas as he once wrote in the *Provincetown Playbill:*

> The theatre of the present offers to the creative artist an undreamed of opportunity, if he can grasp it, to discover the movements of the titanic forces that urge and guide our own time, and reveal them to his fellow men in the flux and flow of life on the stage.

To other producers—until the light rehearsal came along—Jones may have seemed what is stupidly called a "typical artist." I wish that Jones had lived to read a brilliant attack on this popular notion that creativeness somehow involves "temperament" or irresponsible eccentricity. In the *Report of a Committee on the Visual Arts at Harvard University,* an anonymous faculty member wrote:

> The contemporary artist . . . is assumed to be a flighty, unpredictable person, something of a blemish upon his own productions. . . . The work of genius may be the keystone of our civilization, but it takes little persuasion to believe that the genius himself is uncivilized. . . . One need only think responsibly to realize the absurdity of such a view. . . . Art is the epitome of order, the very negation of disorder. . . . So much labor, suffering, discipline, skill, and talent go into a work of artistic creation that we may take it as a truism that the artist is in every sense the master of his product—that if the art is great, the artist necessarily is greater. . . . The artist is a creative individual, the great artist great both as artist and as intellectual.

I want to stress as forcefully as I can the ordered efficiency of Robert Edmond Jones. I saw it operate in many ways—not only at light rehearsals, but also in our collaboration on a book called *Conti-nental Stagecraft*, in his work as a stage director, and in his contributions to motion pictures in color.

When Jones and I were gathering material for that book on European production, we both made notes each evening in the theatre, but, while I went sight-seeing in Stockholm, Berlin, or Vienna, Jones sat all morning at his drawing board turning out those consummately accurate and beautiful records of what he had seen.

When Jones joined with Eugene O'Neill and me in reopening the Provincetown Playhouse back in 1923-24, he began by quickly and cheaply redesigning and redecorating the auditorium. He thrust out a forestage between portals that he cut in the proscenium. With shining tin and a circle of bottle tops, he brought a gay distinction to the sconces on the walls of the auditorium.

At the Provincetown, Jones began to assume a responsibility far greater than that of the designer, though linked closely to it—the work of stage direction. Ours was to be an experimental theatre, and the first of our experiments was not merely the production of Strindberg's THE SPOOK SONATA. It was also the launching of Jones as a director. With his usual care and with a modesty rather unusual in men of the theatre, he sought the collaboration and the seasoning of a man who had learned the ropes. With James Light, he directed in the first four months the Strindberg play, a revival of FASHION, and O'Neill's arrangement of THE ANCIENT MARINER. With the next season—when we managed both Provincetown and the Greenwich Village Theatre —Jones was ready to take on, unaided, the complete responsibility of shaping the characterizations of actors, ordering the tempo of scenes, and fusing performances, settings, and lights into an expressive whole. Working with limited resources, he was as methodical as he was brilliant. The rare versatility of the man—as keen for humor and taste as for tragic power—came through in DESIRE UNDER THE ELMS, PATIENCE, MICHEL AUCLAIR, and LOVE FOR LOVE. The last season at the Greenwich, he mastered as much as could be mastered of O'Neill's THE FOUNTAIN and gave complete expression to that most difficult play The Great God Brown.

For all Jones's uncompromising integrity, he had a practical side that came out in certain Provincetown and Greenwich productions and in the two Technicolor films that he designed. He loved the old comedy Fashion with its stylized characters and its naive asides, and he delighted in the audacious wit of Congreve. Yet he let me persuade him that popular songs of the times—in America 1850 and in England 1700 —would add to the gaiety and the success of the two productions.

Jones came to Hollywood in 1933-34 to help me with the production of the first "live action" movie to be shot on the Technicolor film that used three primary colors instead of two. The ever-enterprising Walt Disney had already made a cartoon by this process. The drawings had been photographed in flat, white light, and Technicolor's experts thought that the same kind of illumination should be spread blankly over actors and sets. Jones, however, believed that, in the matter of color photography, the movies had something to learn from the stage. He believed that he could add directional lighting to overall illumination, and that he could increase the dramatic effect as well as the beauty of a scene by using a certain amount of colored light.

To convince the Technicolor authorities, Jones made tests with Nan Sunderland, the wife of the late Walter Huston. He gave her one of those extraordinary headdresses of the fifteenth century called hennins. Through the veilings that fell away from the two peaks of the towering hat, he threw different hues of light from the sides and the back, contrasting with the normal illumination of the face. The effects he achieved in a dozen different shots were extraordinarily beautiful. In another test he experimented with a change of light to match and heighten a change of emotion. He dressed Miss Sunderland in a simple evening gown, had her look down in a mood of unhappiness, and bathed her in a steel-blue light. Then, while the camera continued grinding, the actress changed her mood, and raised her head into a new light that matched the radiance of her face.

The first film "Designed in Light by Robert Edmond Jones," as the screen credit read, was the two-reeler LA CUCARACHA, produced by John Hay Whitney's Pioneer Pictures. Here audiences not only saw true color for the first time in a fiction film, they also found beauty and drama and, beyond that, a curious effect of three dimensions in certain figures. This last was the result of the subtle use of color in directional lighting.

For Whitney we also made the feature BECKY SHARP, in 1935. To this film Jones brought beautiful costumes and striking sets, but he was unable to contribute as much to the composition and lighting of the people. The director of LA CUCARACHA, Lloyd Corrigan, had welcomed Jones's counsel in the directing of the film and made the most of the series of crayon sketches that Jones prepared for the various camera set-ups. The director of BECKY SHARP, Rouben Mamoulian, who had staged PORGY with such colorful brilliance in New York, felt that he needed little more than Jones's designs and sketches. Yet the effectiveness of many a scene—including Mamoulian's remarkable shooting and editing of the Brussells Ball and the panic that seized upon the dancers as the battle of Waterloo began—was heightened by the vivid beauty of Jones's work.

It was Hollywood's loss that after one more film, THE DANCING PIRATE, it never again employed this distinguished artist even for his designs. It was Broadway's loss that it did not use him as a director in any significant new production after his work with O'Neill in 1926.

RALPH PENDLETON

ROBERT EDMOND JONES: A CHRONOLOGY

THE FOLLOWING CHRONOLOGY includes a list of the various plays, masques, operas, ballets, films, musical comedies, and other theatrical enterprises with which Jones was associated as designer, director, or producer. It also includes his publications, his major New York exhibitions, his principal projects, and a few entries of a purely biographical nature.

For each of his productions the following details, if available, have been provided: the producer for whom the designs were made; a clue as to the complexity of the designer's problem in terms of the number of full settings required or, in plays of many scenes, the general type of production scheme employed; the director; the starred and featured actors—stars indicated by italics; and, for New York productions, the theatre where the production opened and (in parentheses) the number of performances of the New York run. This is the general scheme of organization; the reasons for the numerous deviations from it will be apparent.

Presenting the available information concerning Jones's various projects has proved to be a most intricate problem. In the first place, "project" is certainly one of the most ambiguous terms in the theatrical designer's vocabulary: it may refer to a design made with no thought of a specific production in mind; it may refer to designs for a specific production which was cancelled *before* rehearsals began; it may refer to a production which was cancelled *after* rehearsals began; or it may refer to a production from which the designer withdrew and for which another designer took over. Jones's work provides examples of all these variations of the term. Moreover, with Jones, the problem is complicated further by the fact that the present location of many of his designs is unknown and by the even more frustrating fact that a number of his available designs are undated. In an attempt to resolve this confusion, the term "project" is employed only for designs which were made, as far as can be determined, with no thought of a specific production in mind; and each undated project is entered in the chronology at the point of the earliest reference to it which could be found.

It must be recognized, of course, that Jones made designs which have not survived for projects which are not recorded. (Rose Bogdanoff, Jones's assistant for so many years, told of an afternoon when, at Jones's order and with Jones standing by to supervise the process, she destroyed a series of magnificent designs for productions he had planned for the Radio City Music Hall.)

It is the hope of the compiler that this chronology not only will be useful as reference material, but also will demonstrate the remarkable extent to which the history of Robert Edmond Jones is the history of the American theatre of his time.

ROBERT EDMOND JONES was born on December 12, 1887, in Milton, New Hampshire. After graduating in 1905 from Nute High School, he entered Harvard University in the fall of 1906 as a member of the class of 1910. He graduated *cum laude* with his class, and then remained at Harvard for two years, first as graduate assistant and then as an instructor in the Department of Fine Arts.

In 1912 he left Harvard for New York and a series of small jobs including a brief period as a costume designer on the staff of Comstock and Gest. Then, with the financial assistance of "The Robert Edmond Jones Transportation and Development Company," to which John Reed, Kenneth Macgowan, and others of his friends contributed, he went to Europe.

In the summer of 1913 he was in Florence, where he designed his famous project for Shelley's THE CENCI. He then went to Berlin for a year of informal study and observation at Max Reinhardt's DEUTSCHES THEATER.

With the outbreak of World War I, he returned to New York early in November, 1914.

1914–1915 *Season*

Exhibited several drawings, including designs for THE MERCHANT OF VENICE, in an exhibition of the art of the theatre arranged by the Stage Society of New York for the benefit of the Committee of Mercy. Opened on November 9 at 714 Fifth Avenue.

Published "Stage Lighting: Its Interpretive Power in the Theatre Illustrated" in *The New York Times* for November 21 (12:5). [A letter explaining the method employed to light the plaster cyclorama in a stage model on view at the Stage Society's exhibition, with speculations on the expressive possibilities of this technique for the American theatre.]

Late in the fall of 1914, Jones improvised a setting for the first production of the Washington Square Players, THE GLITTERING GATE by Lord Dunsany. The performance was given in the back room of the Washington Square Bookshop on a small platform for an audience of about 40 at an admission charge of twenty-five cents. Eventually the Washington Square Players were to become The Theatre Guild.

THE MAN WHO MARRIED A DUMB WIFE   A play in one act by Anatole France. Translated by Curtis Hidden Page.

> Originally designed for the Stage Society of New York. 1 setting. Produced by Harley Granville-Barker and Lillah McCarthy. Directed by Mr. Granville-Barker. Music arranged by Cecil Sharp. Wallack's Theatre. January 27. [Performed in repertory as a curtain-raiser for Bernard Shaw's ANDROCLES AND THE LION. The American premières of both plays.]

INTERIOR   A play in one act by Maurice Maeterlinck.

> Designed anonymously for the Washington Square Players. 1 setting. Directed by Edward Goodman. Produced on February 19 in the opening bill of a season of one-act plays at the Bandbox Theatre. Repeat performances.

The Provincetown Players began their career with two one-act plays, SUPRESSED DESIRES by George Cram Cook and Susan Glaspell, and CONSTANCY by Neith Boyce. They "were given at Hutchins Hapgood's house. The stage was set by Jones, who used the veranda with the ocean behind for the first play, and, by the simple expedient of asking the audience to turn its chairs about, the broad doorway at the opposite end of the room for the second. The Hapgood house was crowded for that first performance, and so a deserted old fish house on a wharf, owned by Mary Heaton Vorse, was sketchily renovated with fish nets and circus benches, and the performance was repeated." (Helen Deutsch and Stella Hanau, *The Provincetown: A Story of the Theatre*. New York: Farrar & Rinehart, Inc., 1931, p. 8.)

THE DEVIL'S GARDEN   A play in 4 acts by Edith Ellis. From the novel by William B. Maxwell.

> Designed for Arthur Hopkins. 4 settings. Directed by Mr. Hopkins. Harris Theatre. December 28. (23)

1915–1916 *Season*

CALIBAN BY THE YELLOW SANDS   A community masque of the art of the theatre by Percy Mackaye.

Designed with Joseph Urban for the New York City Shakespeare Tercentenary Celebration. Directed by Mr. Urban and Richard Orynski. Music by Arthur Farwell. [Cast of 1,500, including John Drew, Augustin Duncan, Isadora Duncan, Robert Mantell, Edith Wynne Matthison, Margaret Wycherly.] Lewissohn Stadium of City College. May 24. (10)

[Jones had been invited to design the ten "inner scenes" and the interlude costumes. Because of the sudden illness of the chief costumer, he also designed and supervised the execution of an additional 3,000 costumes within a period of six weeks.

The published version of the play (New York: Doubleday, Page & Company, 1916) is illustrated with designs for the production by Jones and Urban.]

1916–1917

THE HAPPY ENDING   A comedy in 3 acts by Jean and La du Rocher Macpherson.

Designed for Arthur Hopkins. 8 settings. Directed by Mr. Hopkins. Music by Eugen Haile. Shubert Theatre. August 21. (16)

THE MERRY DEATH   A harlequinade in one act by Nicholas Evreinov. Translated by C. E. Bechhofer.

Designed for the Washington Square Players. 1 setting. Costumes designed by George Wolfe Plank. Directed by Philip Moeller. Produced on October 2 in the opening bill of the Washington Square Players' first season at the Comedy Theatre.

TIL EULENSPIEGEL   A ballet by Vaslav Nijinski to the music of Richard Strauss.

Designed for Serge Diaghileff, in association with the Metropolitan Opera Association. 1 setting. Choreography by Nijinski. [With Nijinski as *Til.*] Manhattan Opera House. October 23. (4)

[Jones also made designs for MEPHISTO WALTZ, a ballet by Nijinski to the music of

Franz Liszt, which was to have been produced with TIL EULENSPIEGEL as the two novelties of Nijinski's New York season. The production was cancelled.]

GOOD GRACIOUS ANNABELLE A play in 3 acts by Clare Kummer.

> Designed for Arthur Hopkins. 3 settings. Directed by Mr. Hopkins. With Lola Fisher, May Vokes, Walter Hampden, Edward Nicander. Republic Theatre. October 31. (111)
>
> > Published "The Decorator" in *The New York Times* for December 10 (II:6:3).

A SUCCESSFUL CALAMITY A play in 2 acts by Clare Kummer.

> Designed for Arthur Hopkins. 2 settings. Directed by Mr. Hopkins. With *William Gillette*. Booth Theatre. February 5. (144)

THE RIDER OF DREAMS, a comedy
GRANNY MAUMEE, a tragedy
SIMON THE CYRENIAN, a Passion interlude Three one-act plays for a Negro theatre by Ridgely Torrence.

> Designed for Emilie Hapgood. Directed by Mr. Jones. With the Colored Players. Garden Theatre. April 5. (28) [Jones's first professional assignment as a director.]

Costume sketch for
CALIBAN BY THE
YELLOW SANDS, 1916

CALIBAN BY THE YELLOW SANDS *(Revival)*

> Produced in the Harvard Stadium for the benefit of the Red Cross and the R. O. T. C. Stage designed by Frederick Stanhope and Thomas D'Arcy Brophy. Directed by Mr. Stanhope, assisted by Irving Pichel. Director of the Dance, Virginia Tanner. July 2-21. [Because of the success of the production, the announced run of two weeks was extended to three. Although the costumes and properties of the New York production were used, Jones redesigned the scenery to fit a radically different stage arrangement.]

THE DELUGE A drama in 3 acts by Henning Berger. Adapted from the Swedish by Frank Allen.

Designed for Arthur Hopkins. 1 setting. Directed by Mr. Hopkins. Hudson Theatre. August 20. (16)

THE RESCUING ANGEL   A play in 3 acts by Clare Kummer.

Designed for Arthur Hopkins and Florenz Ziegfeld, Jr. 3 settings. Directed by Mr. Hopkins. With *Billie Burke*. Hudson Theatre. October 8. (32)

Illustrated THE ROLL CALL: A MASQUE OF THE RED CROSS FOR COMMUNITY ACTING AND SINGING by Percy Mackaye (Washington, D. C.: National Headquarters, American Red Cross, 1918). [A special performance, designed by Jones and directed by Irving Pichel, was planned for November in Washington, but it was apparently cancelled. Jones's illustrations consist of a ground-plan, designs for the setting and 2 tableaux, 15 costume designs, and 12 designs for insignia.]

Illustrated THE EVERGREEN TREE: A MASQUE OF CHRISTMAS TIME FOR COMMUNITY SINGING AND ACTING by Percy Mackaye (New York: D. Appleton and Company, 1917). [Jones's illustrations consist of 7 designs for the grouping of actors, a ground-plan, and 26 costume designs.]

THE WILD DUCK   A drama in 5 acts by Henrik Ibsen.

Designed for Arthur Hopkins. 1 setting. Directed by Mr. Hopkins. With *Nazimova*. Plymouth Theatre. March 11. (32) [The first New York production of the play in English. The program credits only the "Studio Setting" to Jones, but newspaper advertisements read "Settings by Robert E. Jones."]

HEDDA GABLER   A drama in 4 acts by Henrik Ibsen.

Designed for Arthur Hopkins. 1 setting. Directed by Mr. Hopkins. With *Nazimova*. Plymouth Theatre. April 8. (24)

Jones was a member of the production staff of a company assembled by Russell Janney for a seven-week season of summer stock (June 3–July 20) at the Pabst Theatre in Milwaukee.

The plays produced were: *(First Week)* Zoë Akins's one-act melodrama, THE MAGICAL CITY, and Bernard Shaw's FANNY'S FIRST PLAY; *(Second Week)* George Du Maurier's TRILBY; *(Third and Fourth Weeks)* Edward Sheldon's THE GARDEN OF PARADISE, a dramatization of Hans Christian Andersen's *The Little Mermaid;* *(Fifth Week)* A "Musical Pictorial Prelude," THE LITTLE SHEPHERD, to the music of Claude Debussy, and Oscar Wilde's AN IDEAL HUSBAND; *(Sixth and Seventh Weeks)* Charlotte Thompson's HEMPFIELD, from the novel by David Grayson.

Scenery designed by Jones, painted by Robert W. Bergman, and lighted by Norman Bel Geddes. Plays directed by Jones, Clifford Brooke, and Oscar Eagle. "Company of 28" included Constance Collier, John L. Shine, Alice Augarde Butler, Alexander Onslow, Frank Sylvester, Irene Haisman, Edward Elton, James Finney, Cathleen Nesbitt, Julien L'Estrange, Gilda Varesi, Wallis Clark, Walter Lewis, Dorothy Chesmond, Malcolm Moreley, J. P. Hagin, Cecil Yapp.

REDEMPTION ("The Living Corpse")   A play in 2 acts by Leo Tolstoi.

> Designed for Arthur Hopkins. 9 settings. Directed by Mr. Hopkins. With *John Barrymore*. Plymouth Theatre. October 3. (204)

BE CALM, CAMILLA   A comedy in 2 acts by Clare Kummer.

> Designed for Arthur Hopkins. 3 settings. Directed by Mr. Hopkins. With Lola Fisher, Walter Hampden, Carlotta Monterey, William Sampson, Hedda Hopper, Arthur Shaw, Rex McDougall. Booth Theatre. October 31. (84)

THE GENTILE WIFE   A play in 4 acts by Rita Wellman.

> Designed for Arthur Hopkins. 3 settings. Directed by Mr. Hopkins. With *Emily Stevens*. Vanderbilt Theatre. December 24. (31)

GUIBOUR   A 14th-century French miracle play. English version by Anna Sprague MacDonald.

> Designed for The Neighborhood Playhouse. Scenery and costumes executed under the direction of Ethel Frankau, Aline Bernstein, and Carmine Vitolo by the workshop classes of The Neighborhood Playhouse. With *Yvette Guilbert*. The Neighbor-

hood Playhouse. January 18 [the first of a series of week-end performances]. (20)

[On March 1, 1922, Mme. Guilbert revived the production for five performances at the 39th Street Theatre.]

Exhibited 8 designs and a model for Galsworthy's STRIFE in an exhibition, *American Stage Designs,* at the Bourgeois Galleries, April 5-26. [The catalogue contains a short essay by Jones, "Fashion in the Theatre," reprinted from *Theatre Arts Magazine* for April (III, p. 115). The Jones designs include an unidentifiable item, SABRINA.]

THE JEST   A drama in 4 acts. Adapted by Edward Sheldon from the Italian of Sem Benelli's LA CENA DELLE BEFFE.

Designed for Arthur Hopkins. 3 settings. Directed by Mr. Hopkins. With *John and Lionel Barrymore.* Plymouth Theatre. April 9. (179)

THE WILL OF SONG   A two-day dramatic service of community singing by Percy Mackaye, in co-operation with Harry Barnhart.

[Jones designed the costumes, using oilcloth as his principal material.] Directed by Irving Pichel. The Armory, Orange, New Jersey. May 2–3.

1919–1920

THE BIRTHDAY OF THE INFANTA   A ballet-pantomime in 2 scenes with music by John Alden Carpenter. Adapted by the composer from the story by Oscar Wilde.

Designed for the Chicago Opera Association. 2 settings. Choreography by Adolph Bolm. [Produced in Chicago earlier in the season, it was given a single New York performance at the Lexington Theatre on February 23. Ruth Page danced *The Infanta.*]

GEORGE WASHINGTON: THE MAN WHO MADE US   A ballad play in
3 acts and a prologue by Percy Mackaye.

Produced by Walter Hampden. 4 settings. Directed by J. Harry
Irvine and Mr. Mackaye. Music arranged by Elliott Schenck.
With *Walter Hampden,* George Marion. Lyric Theatre. March
1. (16)

[Arthur Hopkins had planned to produce the play with Jones's
designs during the 1918-1919 season; but the production was
cancelled because the commercial values of the play, it was felt,
had been jeopardized by the signing of the Armistice. Several
of Jones's designs are reproduced in the published version (New
York: Alfred A. Knopf, 1919).]

THE TRAGEDY OF RICHARD III   "As depicted by William Shakespeare," with 5 scenes interpolated from HENRY
VI.

Designed for Arthur Hopkins. Variations of a unit setting. Cos-
tumes executed by Mme. E. S. Freisinger from designs by Mr.
Jones. Directed by Mr. Hopkins. With *John Barrymore.* Plymouth
Theatre. March 6. (27)

Figure, after Callot,
drawn for *Theatre Arts
Magazine* cover, 1917

Published "A Master" [a tribute to Carl
Sanden, Director of the Eagle Theatre in
Copenhagen] in *The New Republic* for
March 10 (XXII: pp. 52–53).

Exhibited 38 drawings, 9 photographs, and
3 models from various of his productions
at the Bourgeois Galleries, May 1–22, in the
first one-man show to be given an American scene designer. [The exhibition also
included the following projects: 6 designs
for Shelley's THE CENCI made in Italy in the
summer of 1913 (See Jones's essay, "Six
Drawings for The Cenci," in *Theatre Arts
Monthly* for June, 1924 (VIII: pp. 408–
409), in which he assigns them incorrectly
to "the summer of 1912."); 2 scene designs
and a model for Shakespeare's MUCH ADO
ABOUT NOTHING; a model for Materlinck's
THE SEVEN PRINCESSES; and a design for an

1919–1920 *Season*

episode in a community drama, THE SONG OF ROLAND: *A Castle*. The catalogue also lists an unidentifiable item, THE LOVERS.]

1920–1921

SAMSON AND DELILAH   A tragi-comedy in 3 acts by Sven Lange. Translated by Samuel S. Grossman.

Designed for Arthur Hopkins. 2 settings. Directed by Mr. Hopkins. With *Ben-Ami*, Pauline Lord. Greenwich Village Theatre. November 17. (143)

MACBETH   A tragedy by William Shakespeare.

Designed for Arthur Hopkins. Expressionistic abstract units. Directed by Mr. Hopkins. Music by Robert Russell Bennett. With *Lionel Barrymore, Julia Arthur*. Apollo Theatre. February 17. (28)

1921–1922

DADDY'S GONE A-HUNTING   A drama in 3 acts by Zoë Akins.

Designed for Arthur Hopkins. 3 settings. Directed by Mr. Hopkins. With *Marjorie Rambeau*. Plymouth Theatre. August 31. (129)

SWORDS   A drama in 4 acts by Sidney Howard.

Designed for Brock Pemberton. 1 setting. Directed by Mr. Pemberton. Music by Donald N. Tweedy. With Clare Eames, José Ruben. National Theatre. September 1. (36)

THE CLAW   A tragedy in 4 acts by Henri Bernstein. English version by Edward Delaney Dunn and Louis Wolheim.

Designed for Arthur Hopkins. 4 settings. Directed by Mr. Hopkins. With *Lionel Barrymore,* Irene Fenwick. Broadhurst Theatre. October 17. (115)

ANNA CHRISTIE   A play in 4 acts by Eugene O'Neill.

Designed for Arthur Hopkins. 3 settings. Directed by Mr. Hopkins. With *Pauline Lord*, George Marion, Frank Shannon. Vanderbilt Theatre. November 2. (177) [Early programs credit only the "Fog Scene" to Jones; later programs read "Settings by Robert Edmond Jones."]

THE MOUNTAIN MAN   A love story in 5 scenes by Clare Kummer.

Designed for Charles L. Wagner. 3 settings. Directed by Miss Kummer and Edward Elsner. With Sidney Blackmer. Maxine Elliott's Theatre. December 12. (163)

THE IDLE INN   A folk tale in 3 acts by Peretz Hirshbein. Adapted by Isaac Goldberg and Louis Wolheim.

Designed for Arthur Hopkins. 3 settings. Directed by Mr. Hopkins. With *Ben-Ami*, Eva MacDonald, Mary Shaw, Joanna Roos, Hubert Druce, Whitford Kane, Edward G. Robinson. Plymouth Theatre. December 20. (25)

THE S. S. TENACITY   A character comedy in 3 acts by Charles Vildrac. English version by Sidney Howard.

Designed for Augustin Duncan. 1 setting. Directed by Mr. Duncan. With Augustin Duncan, George Gaul, Tom Powers, Marguerite Forrest, Jennie Dickerson. Belmont Theatre. January 2. (67) [Performed with St. John Ervine's THE CRITIC as a curtain-raiser.]

Reviewed in *The New York Times* for January 9 (III:2:1) Kenneth Macgowan's *The Theatre of Tomorrow* (New York: Boni and Liveright, 1921). [The frontispiece of the book is Jones's design for Debussy's opera, PELLÉAS ET MÉLISANDE: *Act IV, Scene III, The Fountain.*]

THE DELUGE (*Revival*)

Produced and directed by Arthur Hopkins. A revival of the 1917 production. Plymouth Theatre. January 27. (45)

THE HAIRY APE   A comedy of ancient and modern life in 8 scenes by Eugene O'Neill.

Designed with Cleon Throckmorton for The Provincetown Players. 7 settings. Directed by James Light and Arthur Hopkins. [With Louis Wolheim.] Provincetown Playhouse. March 9. (108)

1921–1922 *Season*	VOLTAIRE	A romantic comedy in 3 acts by Leila Taylor and Gertrude Purcell.

Designed for Arthur Hopkins. 1 setting. Directed by Mr. Hopkins. With *Arnold Daly*. Plymouth Theatre. March 20. (16)

Traveled for ten weeks with Kenneth Macgowan during April, May, and June. Attended nearly sixty theatrical performances in France, Sweden, Germany, Czechoslovakia, and Austria. Their resulting book, *Continental Stagecraft* (New York: Harcourt, Brace and Company, 1922), is illustrated with 40 plates by Jones, 8 in color.

1922–1923	ROSE BERND	A drama in 3 acts by Gerhart Hauptmann. Adapted by Ludwig Lewissohn.

Designed for Arthur Hopkins. 4 settings. Directed by Mr. Hopkins. With *Ethel Barrymore*. Longacre Theatre. September 26. (87)

	HAMLET	A tragedy by William Shakespeare.

Designed for Arthur Hopkins. Variations of a unit setting. Directed by Mr. Hopkins. With *John Barrymore*. Sam H. Harris Theatre. November 16. (101)

	ROMEO AND JULIET	A tragedy by William Shakespeare.

Designed for Arthur Hopkins. Variations of a unit setting. Directed by Mr. Hopkins. With *Ethel Barrymore*. Longacre Theatre. December 27. (29)

	THE LAUGHING LADY	A comedy in 3 acts by Alfred Sutro.

Designed for Arthur Hopkins. 2 settings. Directed by Mr. Hopkins. With *Ethel Barrymore*. Longacre Theatre. February 12. (96)

LAUNZI ("Heavenly and Earthly Love")   A play in 3 acts by Ferenc
                Molnar. Adapted by Edna St. Vincent Millay.

> Designed for Arthur Hopkins. 5 settings. Directed by Mr. Hop-
> kins. With *Pauline Lord*. Plymouth Theatre. October 10. (13)

A ROYAL FANDANGO   A comedy in 3 acts by Zoë Akins.

> Designed for Arthur Hopkins. 3 settings. Directed by Mr. Hop-
> kins. With *Ethel Barrymore*. Plymouth Theatre. November 12.
> (24)

THE SPOOK SONATA   A play in 3 movements by August Strindberg.
                Translated by Edwin Björkman.

> Designed with Cleon Throckmorton for The Experimental The-
> atre, Inc. 3 settings. Directed by James Light and Mr. Jones.
> Masks by James Light. Buddha and statue executed by Remo
> Bufano. Costumes executed by Kirah Markham. [With Clare
> Eames as guest-player.] Provincetown Playhouse. January 5. (24)

> [With this production, control of The Provincetown Playhouse
> passed from The Provincetown Players to a new producing group
> called The Experimental Theatre, Inc., headed by Kenneth Mac-
> gowan, Robert Edmond Jones, and Eugene O'Neill. They organ-
> ized a permanent acting company of ten, augmented by "guest-
> players" and actors engaged for specific productions. During the
> following season, they operated both The Provincetown Play-
> house and The Greenwich Village Theatre.]

Signet of the
Greenwich Village Theatre
probably about 1924

THE LIVING MASK ("Henry IV")   A satirical comedy in 3 acts by
                Luigi Pirandello. Translated by Arthur Living-
                ston.

> Designed for Brock Pemberton. 2 settings. Directed by Mr. Pem-
> berton. With Arnold Korff. 44th Street Theatre. January 21. (28)

FASHION, OR LIFE IN NEW YORK   A comedy in 3 acts by Anna Cora
                Mowatt. Acting version, with songs of the pe-
                riod [1845], arranged by Brian Hooker and
                Deems Taylor.

1923–1924 *Season*

Produced by The Experimental Theatre, Inc. Scenery by Reginald Marsh, Cleon Throckmorton, and Mr. Jones. Costumes by Kirah Markham and Mr. Jones. Directed by James Light and Mr. Jones. [With Clare Eames as guest-player.] Provincetown Playhouse. February 3. [More than 152 performances.]

WELDED   A play in 3 acts by Eugene O'Neill.

Designed for Macgowan, Jones, and O'Neill (producing independently), in association with the Selwyns. 3 settings. Directed by Stark Young. With *Doris Keane, Jacob Ben-Ami.* 39th Street Theatre. March 17. (24)

GEORGE DANDIN, OR THE HUSBAND CONFOUNDED   A comedy in 3 acts by Molière. Translated by Stark Young.

Designed with Cleon Throckmorton for The Experimental Theatre, Inc. 1 setting. Directed by Mr. Young. On a double bill with:

THE ANCIENT MARINER   A dramatic arrangement by Eugene O'Neill of the poem by Samuel Taylor Coleridge.

Designed by Mr. Jones. Masks by James Light. Directed by Mr. Jones and Mr. Light. Provincetown Playhouse. April 16. (33)

Published "Notes on the Theatre" in *Theatre Arts Monthly* for May (VIII: pp. 323–325).

AT THE GATEWAY   "A profane mystery" in one act by Luigi Pirandello.

Designed for a charity performance for the benefit of the blind at the Imperial Theatre on Sunday, May 4. [No information available as to whether it actually took place.]

THE EMPEROR JONES   A play in 8 scenes by Eugene O'Neill.

Produced by The Experimental Theatre, Inc. [A revival of the 1920 production by The Provincetown Players. With Paul Robeson as guest-player.] Directed by James Light. Settings by Cleon Throckmorton. Provincetown Playhouse. May 5.

HEDDA GABLER   A drama in 4 acts by Henrik Ibsen.

Designed for The Equity Players, Inc. by Woodman Thompson. Directed by Mr. Jones. With Dudley Digges, Fritz Leiber, Clare Eames, Roland Young, Margalo Gillmore, Augusta Haviland, Helen Van Hoose. 48th Street Theatre. [A series of special matinees beginning May 16.] (6)

ALL GOD'S CHILLUN GOT WINGS   A play in 2 acts by Eugene O'Neill.

Produced by The Experimental Theatre, Inc. [With Paul Robeson as guest-player.] Directed by James Light. Settings by Cleon Throckmorton. Provincetown Playhouse. May 26.

THE CRIME IN THE WHISTLER ROOM   A play in 3 acts by Edmund Wilson.

Produced by Experimental Theatre, Inc. Directed by Stanley Howlett. Settings by Cleon Throckmorton. Incidental music composed and arranged by Macklin Marrow. Provincetown Playhouse. October 9. (25)

THE SAINT   A drama in 3 acts by Stark Young.

Designed for Experimental Theatre, Inc. 2 settings. Directed by Richard Boleslawsky, Mr. Young, and Mr. Jones. Incidental music composed and arranged by Macklin Marrow. [With Leo Carillo and Maria Ouspenskaya as guest-players.] Greenwich Village Theatre. October 11. (17) [This production was Ouspenskaya's début in English and her first performance outside the Moscow Art Theatre.]

S. S. GLENCAIRN   Four episodes of the sea by Eugene O'Neill.

Produced by Experimental Theatre, Inc. Directed by James Light. Settings by Cleon Throckmorton. Provincetown Playhouse. November 3. (105)

DESIRE UNDER THE ELMS   A drama in 3 parts by Eugene O'Neill.

Designed for Experimental Theatre, Inc. Simultaneous setting. Directed by Mr. Jones. [With Mary Morris of the permanent company as *Abbie Putnam*, and Walter Huston, guest-player, as *Ephraim Cabot*.] Greenwich Village Theatre. November 11. (208)

PATIENCE, OR BUNTHORNE'S BRIDE   A comic opera in 2 acts by W. S. Gilbert and Arthur Sullivan.

Designed with Cleon Throckmorton, in the manner of E. Burne-Jones, for Experimental Theatre, Inc. 2 settings. Directed by Mr. Jones. Musical Director and Conductor, Macklin Marrow. Provincetown Playhouse. December 29. (104)

BEYOND   A drama in 5 acts and 22 scenes by Walter Hasenclever. Translated by Rita Matthias.

Designed for Experimental Theatre, Inc. Directed by James Light. [With the cast of two characters played by Helen Gahagan, guest-player, and Walter Abel of the permanent company.] Provincetown Playhouse. January 26. (16)

THE TRIUMPH OF THE EGG   A comedy in one act by Sherwood Anderson and Raymond O'Neil.

Produced by Experimental Theatre, Inc. Directed by James Light. Settings by Cleon Throckmorton. On a double bill with:

DIFF'RENT   A play in 2 acts by Eugene O'Neill.

[A revival of the 1920 production by The Provincetown Players.] Directed by Helen Freeman. Settings by Cleon Throckmorton. Provincetown Playhouse. February 10. (22)

MICHEL AUCLAIR   A play in 3 acts by Charles Vildrac.

Designed after sketches by M. Vildrac for Experimental Theatre, Inc. 2 settings, executed by Cleon Throckmorton. Directed by Mr. Jones. Provincetown Playhouse. March 4. (19)

LOVE FOR LOVE   A comedy in 4 acts by William Congreve.

Designed for Experimental Theatre, Inc. Variations of a permanent setting. Costumes designed by Millia Davenport and Mr. Jones. Directed by Mr. Jones. Greenwich Village Theatre. March 31. (63)

RUINT   A folk comedy in 3 acts by Hatcher Hughes.

Produced by Experimental Theatre, Inc. Directed by James Light. Settings designed and executed by Cleon Throckmorton. Provincetown Playhouse. April 7. (30)

[This production marked the end of Macgowan, Jones, and O'Neill's association with Experimental Theatre, Inc.]

TRELAWNEY OF 'THE WELLS'   A comedietta in 4 acts by Sir Arthur Wing Pinero.

Designed for The Player's Fourth Annual Revival. 3 settings. Directed by William Seymour. With an all-star cast. Knickerbocker Theatre. Week of June 1. (8)

Published "The Robe of Light" in *Theatre Arts Monthly* for August (IX, pp. 493-99).

OUTSIDE LOOKING IN   A play in 3 acts by Maxwell Anderson. Dramatized from Jim Tully's *Beggars of Life*.

Produced by Macgowan, Jones, and O'Neill. Directed by Augustin Duncan. Designed by Cleon Throckmorton. Greenwich Village Theatre. September 7. (113)

THE BUCCANEER   A romantic comedy in 3 acts by Maxwell Anderson and Laurence Stallings.

Designed for Arthur Hopkins. 2 settings. Directed by Mr. Hopkins. With *William Farnum,* Estelle Winwood. Plymouth Theatre. October 2. (20)

Exhibited 37 designs and a model for LOVE FOR LOVE in a one-man show at the Bourgeois Galleries, October 17-31. [The designs exhibited included the following projects: drawings for Act I and Act II of Alexander Blok's THE STAR; and a design for Shakespeare's As You Like It (possibly for the production which Arthur Hopkins and Ethel Barrymore had considered for her 1922–1923 season at the Longacre Theatre?). They also included three costume designs for Melchior Lengyel's THE KINGDOM OF SANCHO PANZA, which, adapted by Sidney Howard under the title SANCHO PANZA, was produced in 1923 by Russell Janney and Emilie Hapgood with designs by James Reynolds and Reginald Marsh.]

During 1925 Jones apparently designed the Uraneff production of Blok's THE SHOW BOOTH; but his designs were accidentally destroyed, and no other information seems to be available.

Published *Drawings for the Theatre* (New York: Theatre Arts, Inc., 1925) with an Introduction by Arthur Hopkins, a Preface by Jones, and 35 plates. [Plate Five, LA CENA DELLE BEFFE: *Act II, Ginevra's Chamber,* was designed for an opera composed by Umberto Giordano with libretto adapted by Sem Benelli from his play of the same title. This drawing, markedly different from Jones's design for the corresponding scene in THE JEST (1919), was rejected by the Metropolitan Opera Association, which produced Giordano's work during the 1925–1926 season with designs by Joseph Urban.]

THE LAST NIGHT OF DON JUAN   A play in prologue and 2 acts by Edmond Rostand. Translated by Sidney Howard.

Produced by Macgowan, Jones, and O'Neill. Directed by Robert Milton. Designed by James Reynolds. Musical score arranged by Macklin Marrow from Mozart's DON GIOVANNI. With Augustin Duncan, Violet Kemble Cooper. On a double bill with:

THE PILGRIMAGE   A play in one act by Charles Vildrac. Translated by Sigourney Thayer.

Directed by Augustin Duncan. Greenwich Village Theatre. November 9. (16)

IN A GARDEN   A comedy in 3 acts by Philip Barry.

Designed for Arthur Hopkins. 1 setting. Directed by Mr. Hopkins. With *Laurette Taylor*, Frank Conroy, Louis Calhern. Plymouth Theatre. November 16. (73)

THE FOUNTAIN   A play in 11 scenes by Eugene O'Neill.

Designed for Macgowan, Jones, and O'Neill. 8 settings. Directed by Mr. Jones. [With Walter Huston.] Greenwich Village Theatre. December 10. (28)

During 1925, Jones worked on designs for Shakespeare's MUCH ADO ABOUT NOTHING for The Theatre Guild. The production, which was to have starred Alfred Lunt and Lynn Fontanne, was cancelled.

THE GREAT GOD BROWN   A play in prologue, 4 acts, and epilogue by Eugene O'Neill.

Designed for Macgowan, Jones, and O'Neill. 8 settings. Directed by Mr. Jones. With William Harrigan, Robert Keith, Leona Hogarth, Anne Shoemaker. Greenwich Village Theatre. January 23. (171)

LITTLE EYOLF   A drama in 3 acts by Henrik Ibsen.

Produced by William A. Brady, Jr. and Dwight Deere Wiman. [Costumes for Clare Eames as *Mrs. Rita Allmers* and Margalo Gillmore as *Miss Asta Allmers* designed by Jones; other costumes and settings designed by Jo Mielziner.] Guild Theatre. Special matinees beginning February 2. (8)

THE JEST (*Revival*)

Produced and directed by Arthur Hopkins. [A revival of the 1919 production.] With Basil Sydney, Violet Heming, Alphonz Ethier. Plymouth Theatre. February 4. (77)

SKYSCRAPERS
A ballet of modern American life in 6 scenes by John Alden Carpenter.

Designed for the Metropolitan Opera Association. 5 settings. "*Mise-en-scène*" by Mr. Carpenter and Mr. Jones. Choreography by Samuel Lee. Metropolitan Opera House. February 19. [On a triple bill with Puccini's GIANNI SCHICCHI and Leoncavallo's PAGLIACCI.] (4)

BRIDE OF THE LAMB
A play in 3 acts by William J. Hurlbut.

Produced by Macgowan, Jones, and O'Neill, in association with Robert Milton. Directed by Mr. Milton. Designed by Cleon Throckmorton. With *Alice Brady*. Greenwich Village Theatre. March 30. (89)

1926–1927

MARTINE
A play in 3 acts by Jean-Jacques Bernard.

Designed for the American Laboratory Theatre. Directed by Richard Boleslavsky. American Laboratory Theatre. April 3. (16)

Awarded the Howland Memorial Medal by Yale University on April 25.

1927–1928

Published "The Theatre As It Has Been and As It Is" in *Theatre Arts Monthly* for September (XI: pp. 661–73); revised and reprinted (1941) as Chapter III in *The Dramatic Imagination.*

Published "Art in the Theatre" in *The Yale Review* for October (XVII: pp. 37–48); revised and reprinted (1941) as Chapter II in *The Dramatic Imagination.*

THE HOUSE OF WOMEN
A play in 3 acts by Louis Bromfield. Dramatized by Mr. Bromfield from his novel, *The Green Bay Tree.*

Designed for Arthur Hopkins. 1 setting. Directed by Mr. Hopkins. With *Elsie Ferguson, Nance O'Neil.* Maxine Elliott's Theatre. October 3. (40)

PARIS BOUND   A comedy in 3 acts by Philip Barry.

Designed for Arthur Hopkins. 2 settings. Directed by Mr. Hopkins. With *Madge Kennedy.* Music Box Theatre. December 27. (234)

During 1927, Jones designed as a project D'Annunzio's LA GIOCONDA: Act III, *Anteroom of the Sculptor's Studio.*

FAUST   An opera in 4 acts, with music by Charles Gounod and with a new text in English by Robert A. Simon from the French adapters of Goethe's German poem.

Designed for the American Opera Company. 6 settings. Conducted by Frank St. Leger. Gallo Theatre. January 10. (15)

SALVATION   A play in 3 acts by Sidney Howard and Charles MacArthur.

Designed for Arthur Hopkins. 3 settings. Directed by Mr. Hopkins. With *Pauline Lord,* Osgood Perkins. Empire Theatre. January 31. (31)

Published "The Artist's Approach to the Theatre" in *Theatre Arts Monthly* for September (XII: pp. 629–34).

MACHINAL   A play in 2 parts and 10 episodes by Sophie Treadwell.

Designed for Arthur Hopkins. Variations of a unit setting. Directed by Mr. Hopkins. Occasional music by Frank Harling. With Zita Johann. Plymouth Theatre. September 7. (91)

MR. MONEYPENNY   A verbal cartoon in 3 acts by Channing Pollock.

> Designed for Mr. Pollock. Directed by Richard Boleslavsky. Liberty Theatre. October 17. (61)

THESE DAYS   A play in 3 acts by Katharine Clugston.

> Designed for Arthur Hopkins. 5 settings. Directed by Mr. Hopkins. [With Mary Hall, Katharine Hepburn, Helen Freeman, Mildred McCoy.] Cort Theatre. November 12. (8)

HOLIDAY   A comedy in 3 acts by Philip Barry.

> Designed for Arthur Hopkins. 2 settings. Directed by Mr. Hopkins. With Hope Williams. Plymouth Theatre. November 26. (229)

SERENA BLANDISH, OR THE DIFFICULTY OF GETTING MARRIED   A fabulous comedy in 2 acts and 10 scenes by S. N. Behrman, based on the novel of the same name by "A Lady of Quality."

> Designed for Jed Harris. 6 settings. Directed by Mr. Harris. With Ruth Gordon, Constance Collier, A. E. Matthews. Morosco Theatre. January 23. (93)

BECKY SHARP   A play in 4 acts by Langdon Mitchell. Founded on Thackeray's *Vanity Fair*.

> Designed for The Players' Eighth Annual Revival. 4 settings. Directed by Dudley Digges. With an all-star cast. Knickerbocker Theatre. Week of June 3. (8)

1929–1930

SEE NAPLES AND DIE   An extravagant comedy in 3 acts by Elmer Rice.

> Designed for Lewis E. Gensler. 1 setting. Directed by Mr. Rice. With Claudette Colbert, Roger Pryor, Pedro de Cordoba, Beatrice Herford. Vanderbilt Theatre. September 26. (62)

LADIES LEAVE   A comedy in 3 acts by Sophie Treadwell.

Designed for Charles Hopkins. 1 setting. Directed by Mr. Hopkins. With *Henry Hull, Walter Connolly*. Charles Hopkins Theatre. October 1. (15)

YOLANDA OF CYPRUS   An opera in 3 acts by Clarence Loomis. Libretto by Cale Young Rice.

Designed for the American Opera Company. 3 settings. Majestic Theatre, Chicago. October 9. (4)

THE CHANNEL ROAD   A comedy in 3 acts by Alexander Woollcott and George S. Kaufman. Suggested by Maupassant's *Boule de Suif*.

Designed for Arthur Hopkins. 1 setting. Directed by Mr. Hopkins. Plymouth Theatre. October 17. (60)

WEEK-END   A play in 3 acts by Austin Parker.

Designed for Bela Blau, Inc. 1 setting. Directed by Worthington Miner. With Vivienne Osborne. John Golden Theatre. October 22. (11)

SEVEN YEAR LOVE   A comedy in 3 acts by John D. Haggart.

Designed for Brock Pemberton. Directed by Antoinette Perry and Mr. Pemberton. Tried out in Washington and Baltimore during October. Production cancelled.

CROSS ROADS   A drama in 3 acts by Martin Flavin.

Designed for Lewis E. Gensler. 3 settings. Directed by Guthrie McClintic. With Sylvia Sidney, Eric Dressler. Morosco Theatre. November 11. (28)

Published "Theory of Modern Production," a section of the article on *Theatre* in the 14th edition of the *Encyclopaedia Britannica* (1929); revised and reprinted (1941) as Chapter I in *The Dramatic Imagination*.

A tailpiece for
Marc Connelly's
The Green Pastures, 1930

CHILDREN OF DARKNESS ("The Gaoler's Wench")   A tragi-comedy in 3 acts by Edwin Justus Mayer.

Designed for Kenneth Macgowan and Joseph Verner Reed. 1 setting. Directed by Mr. Mayer. With *Basil Sydney, Mary Ellis.* Biltmore Theatre. January 7. (79)

REBOUND   A comedy in 3 acts by Donald Ogden Stewart.

Designed for Arthur Hopkins. 2 settings. Directed by Mr. Hopkins. With Hope Williams. Plymouth Theatre. February 3. (114)

THE GREEN PASTURES   A fable in 2 parts and 18 scenes by Marc Connelly. Suggested by Roark Bradford's Southern sketches, *Ol' Man Adam an' His Chillun.*

Designed for Laurence Rivers, Inc. Directed by Mr. Connelly. Music under the direction of Hall Johnson. [With Richard B. Harrison as *The Lord.*] Mansfield Theatre. February 26. (640) [For the published version (New York: Farrar & Rinehart, Inc., 1930) Jones designed, in addition to numerous head- and tailpieces, 12 full-page illustrations: *The Death of Moses, The Fish Fry, Adam, The Death of Abel, The Lord Shows Noah His Plan for Building the Ark, The Storm, The Ark on Mount Ararat, The Lord's Office* (2 versions), *Moses and the Burning Bush, The Prayer of Moses, The Vision of Hezdrel.*]

DIE GLÜCKLICHE HAND ("The Hand of Fate")   An opera-pantomime by Arnold Schönberg.

Designed for the League of Composers and the Philadelphia Opera Association. 1 setting. Directed by Rouben Mamoulian. Conducted by Leopold Stokowski. Metropolitan Opera House, Philadelphia, April 11, 12, 14; Metropolitan Opera House, New York, April 22, 23. [The cast included Doris Humphrey as *The Woman* and Charles Weidman as *The Stranger.*] On a double bill with Stravinsky's LE SACRE DU PRINTEMPS [with Martha Graham dancing *The Chosen One*]. The American stage premières of both works.

ROADSIDE   A comedy in 3 acts by Lynn Riggs.

Designed for Arthur Hopkins. 2 settings. Costumes designed by

Everett Shinn. Directed by Mr. Hopkins. With Ralph Bellamy. Longacre Theatre. September 26. (11)

LE PREZIOSE RIDICOLE — A lyric comedy in one act. Based on Molière's LES PRÉCIEUSES RIDICULES. Italian text by Arturo Rossato. Music by Felice Lattuada.

Designed for the Metropolitan Opera Association. 1 setting. Directed by Ernst Lert. Conducted by Vincenzo Bellezza. [With Lucrezia Bori and Gladys Swarthout.] Metropolitan Opera House. December 10. (4) [First performance in this country.] On a double bill with Moussorgsky's THE FAIR AT SOROTCHINTZY.

WOZZECK — An opera in 3 acts and 15 scenes by Alban Berg. German text from the posthumous play by Georg Büchner.

Designed for the Philadelphia Grand Opera Company. Directed by Wilhelm von Wymetal. Conducted by Leopold Stokowski. [With Ivan Ivantzoff as *Wozzeck*.] American première at the Metropolitan Opera House, Philadelphia, March 19. Metropolitan Opera House, New York, November 24. (2)

OEDIPUS REX — An opera-oratorio in 2 acts after Sophocles by Igor Stravinsky. Text by Jean Cocteau translated into Latin by Jean Danielou.

Designed for the League of Composers in association with Leopold Stokowski and the Philadelphia Orchestra. Puppets executed by Remo Bufano. Conducted by Leopold Stokowski. [With Paul Althouse as *Oedipus* and Margaret Matzenauer as *Jocasta*.] Metropolitan Opera House, Philadelphia, April 10, 12, 13; Metropolitan Opera House, New York, April 21, 22. (5) On a double bill with Prokofieff's LE PAS D'ACIER. [The American stage premières of both works.]

Published in *Theatre Arts Monthly* for October (XV, p. 795) a design (project) for Act III of Ibsen's WHEN WE DEAD AWAKEN.

MOURNING BECOMES ELECTRA   A trilogy by Eugene O'Neill.

Designed for The Theatre Guild, Inc. 5 settings. Directed by Philip Moeller. With Alice Brady, Alla Nazimova, Earle Larimore, Lee Baker, Thomas Chalmers. Guild Theatre. October 26. (150)

THE LADY WITH A LAMP   A play in 3 acts by Reginald Berkeley.

Designed for Kenneth Macgowan and Joseph Verner Reed. 6 settings. Directed by Leslie Banks. With *Edith Evans,* Patricia Collinge. Maxine Elliott's Theatre. November 17. (12)

THE PASSING PRESENT   A drama in 3 acts by Gretchen Damrosch.

Designed for Arthur Hopkins. 1 setting. Directed by Mr. Hopkins. With *Hope Williams.* Ethel Barrymore Theatre. December 7. (16)

Exhibited 37 designs, 2 of the Bufano puppets for OEDIPUS REX, and a model for MUCH ADO ABOUT NOTHING, in a one-man show at the Bourgeois Galleries, March 5-26. [The catalogue includes a selected list of 49 of Jones's productions. I have not been able to determine his precise relationship to one of them: J. Frank Davis' THE LADDER (3rd edition).]

NIGHT OVER TAOS   A play in 3 acts by Maxwell Anderson.

Designed for the Group Theatre, Inc. 1 setting. Directed by Lee Strasberg. 48th Street Theatre. March 9. (13)

1932 : *Summer*

CAMILLE   A play in 5 acts by Alexandre Dumas, fils. A new version by Edna and Delos Chappell and Mr. Jones.

Produced, designed, and directed for the First Annual Play Festival of the Central City Opera House Association. 5 settings. With *Lillian Gish,* supported by an "all-star cast." Music composed and arranged by Macklin Marrow. Central City Opera House, Central City, Colorado. July 16–23.

CAMILLE *(Revival)*

The Central City production produced in New York by Delos Chappell, Inc. Morosco Theatre. November 1. (15)

LUCRECE   A play in 6 scenes, translated by Thornton Wilder from André Obey's LE VIOL DE LUCRÈCE.

Designed for Katharine Cornell. Directed by Guthrie McClintic, with special assistance by Martha Graham. Music by Deems Taylor. With Robert Loraine, Blanche Yurka, Brian Aherne, Charles Waldron, Joyce Carey, Pedro de Cordoba, Katharine Cornell. Belasco Theatre. December 20. (31)

INAUGURAL PROGRAM OF THE RADIO CITY MUSIC HALL

[In April, 1932, S. L. ("Roxy") Rothafel announced Jones's appointment as Art Director for the Radio City Music Hall, with the responsibility of designing and supervising the visual side of the productions planned for the vast auditorium. The Inaugural Program on December 27, under the personal direction of "Roxy," was advertised as the "supreme entertainment of the age." It included 48 Roxyettes, the Patricia Bowman Ballet of 80, an orchestra of 90, and a chorus of 100. A gigantic vaudeville show, "Roxy's" opening bill included Weber and Fields as well as Harald Kreutzberg, De Wolf Hopper as well as Martha Graham— and, *very* late in the evening, a condensed version of Bizet's CARMEN with settings and costumes by Robert Edmond Jones.

On January 9 the resignation of Jones was announced.]

PIERROT LUNAIRE   A set of short poems by Albert Giraud, translated into German by Erich Hartleben. Music by Arnold Schönberg.

Designed for the League of Composers. Abstract plastic unit and stylized Pierrot costume. Directed and conducted by Leopold Stokowski. With Mina Hager and an ensemble from the Philadelphia Orchestra. Town Hall. April 16. (1) [Produced on a program with two Russian musical films.]

ENCHANTMENT   A comedy by Laurette Taylor.

Designed and directed for Harry Moses. With Laurette Taylor. Opening scheduled for April 18 at the Plymouth Theatre. Postponed and then cancelled.

Design for program cover of PIERROT LUNAIRE, 1933

1932–1933 *Season*

NINE PINE STREET A play in 6 scenes and an epilogue by John Colton and Carlton Miles. Based on a play by William Miles and Donald Blackwell.

Designed for Margaret Hewes. 1 setting. Directed by A. H. Van Buren. With Lillian Gish. Longacre Theatre. April 27. (28)

Published "Central City's Ghosts Again Eye the Future" in *The New York Times* for June 18 (X:1).

Married Margaret Huston Carrington on June 21, at Greenwich, Connecticut.

1933 : *Summer*

THE MERRY WIDOW An operetta in 3 acts by Franz Lehar.

Produced, designed, and directed for the Second Annual Play Festival of the Central City Opera House Association. 3 settings. With an "all-star cast" including Gladys Swarthout, Natalie Hall, Richard Bonelli. Orchestra conducted by Macklin Marrow. Dances supervised by Russell Lewis. Central City Opera House, Central City, Colorado. August 5–19.

1933–1934

AH, WILDERNESS! A comedy of recollection in 3 acts by Eugene O'Neill.

Designed for The Theatre Guild, Inc. 4 settings. Directed by Philip Moeller. With George M. Cohan. Guild Theatre. October 2. (289)

THE GREEN BAY TREE A play in 3 acts by Mordaunt Shairp.

Designed for Jed Harris, in association with Lee Shubert. 2 settings. Directed by Mr. Harris. Cort Theatre. October 20. (166)

MARY OF SCOTLAND A play in 3 acts by Maxwell Anderson.

Designed for The Theatre Guild, Inc. 5 settings. Directed by Theresa Helburn. With Helen Hayes, Philip Merivale, Helen Menken. Alvin Theatre. November 27. (248)

THE JOYOUS SEASON   A comedy in 3 acts by Philip Barry.   1933–1934 *Season*

> Designed for Arthur Hopkins. 1 setting. Directed by Mr. Hopkins. With Lillian Gish. Belasco Theatre. January 29. (16)

>> Published "The Bard in the Central City Opera House" in *The New York Times* for June 24 (IX:1:3).

OTHELLO   A tragedy by William Shakespeare. Adapted into 2 acts and 9 scenes.   1934 : *Summer*

> Produced, designed, and directed for the Third Annual Play Festival of the Central City Opera House Association. [With Walter Huston as *Othello*, Kenneth MacKenna as *Iago*, Nan Sunderland as *Desdemona*, Helen Freeman as *Emilia*.] Central City Opera House, Central City, Colorado. July 21–August 4.

>> Published "My Hollywood" in *Vanity Fair* for October (43: 37, 64).   1934–1935

DARK VICTORY   A play in 3 acts by George Brewer, Jr. and Bertram Bloch.

> Designed for Alexander McKaig. 3 settings. Directed by Robert Milton. With *Tallulah Bankhead*, Earle Larimore. Plymouth Theatre. November 9. (51)

>> Published "A Revolution in the Movies" in *Vanity Fair* for June (44: 13, 58).

BECKY SHARP   A film in Technicolor adapted from the Langdon Mitchell play, which was based on Thackeray's *Vanity Fair*. Screen play by Francis Edward Faragon.

> A Pioneer Pictures production, distributed by RKO. "Color designs by Robert Edmond Jones." Directed by Rouben Mamoulian. With *Miriam Hopkins*, Billie Burke, Frances Dee, Cedric Hardwicke, Alison Skipworth, Alan Mowbray, Nigel Bruce. First New York run opened on June 13 at the Radio City Music Hall. [Jones's first film, LA CUCARACHA, a short, was released in 1934.]

1935 : *Summer*

Published "Glamour Revived" in *The New York Times* for June 30 (X:1).

CENTRAL CITY NIGHTS   An original musical review.

Produced, designed, and directed for the Fourth Annual Play Festival of the Central City Opera House Association. Orchestra conducted by Frank St. Leger. Dances supervised by Russell Lewis. With an "all-star cast." Central City Opera House, Central City, Colorado. July 6–20.

1935–1936

Contributed to "The Anniversary Post Bag" in *The Yale Review* for September (XXV, pp. 21–23).

Awarded the Fine Arts Medal of the American Institute of Architects, May 4.

THE DANCING PIRATE   A film in Technicolor adapted by Jack Wagner and Boris Ingster from a story by Emma-Lindsay Squier. Screen play by Ray Harris and Francis Faragon. Music and lyrics by Richard Rodgers and Lorenz Hart.

A Pioneer Pictures production, released by RKO. "Designed by Robert Edmond Jones." Directed by Lloyd Corrigan. Produced by John Speaks. First New York run opened on June 17 at the Rivoli Theatre.

1936–1937

Published "The Moor of Venice" in *Stage* for December (XIV, pp. 70–71).

OTHELLO   A tragedy by William Shakespeare.

Designed and directed for Max Gordon. A considerably revised version of his Central City production of 1934. [With Walter Huston as *Othello*, Nan Sunderland as *Desdemona*, Brian Aherne as *Iago*, Natalie Hall as *Emilia*.] New Amsterdam Theatre. January 6. (21)

Published "The Problem of Color" in *The New York Times* for February 27 (X:4:1).

THE SEA GULL   A play in 4 acts by Anton Chekhov. Translated by Stark Young.

Designed for The Theatre Guild, Inc. 3 settings. Directed by Robert Milton. With *Alfred Lunt, Lynn Fontanne,* Richard Whorf, Sydney Greenstreet, Uta Hagen, Edith King, Margaret Webster. Shubert Theatre. March 28. (41)

RUY BLAS   Brian Hooker's adaptation in 4 acts of Victor Hugo's romantic tragedy.

Produced, designed, and directed for the Seventh Annual Play Festival of the Central City Opera House Association. 4 settings. With *Helen Chandler, Bramwell Fletcher,* Nance O'Neil, Percy Waram, William Sauter. Central City Opera House, Central City, Colorado. July 16–30.

EVERYWHERE I ROAM   A play in 3 acts by Arnold Sundgaard and Marc Connelly.

Designed for Bela Blau, Inc., and Mr. Connelly, by arrangement with Robert Porterfield's Barter Theatre. Directed by Mr. Connelly. Songs by Fred Stewart. Choral arrangements and direction by Lehman Engel. Dances directed by Felicia Sorel. With a "cast of 60." National Theatre. December 29. (13)

THE PHILADELPHIA STORY   A comedy in 3 acts by Philip Barry.

Designed for The Theatre Guild, Inc. 2 settings. Directed by Robert B. Sinclair. With Katharine Hepburn, Van Heflin, Joseph Cotten, Nicholas Joy, Shirley Booth. Shubert Theatre. March 28. (417)

THE DEVIL AND DANIEL WEBSTER   A musical folk play by Stephen Vincent Benét and Douglas Moore.

Designed for the American Lyric Theatre in association with the League of Composers. Directed by John Houseman. Conducted by Fritz Reiner. Martin Beck Theatre. May 18. (6) On a double-bill with FILLING STATION, Virgil Thomson's "ballet-document" in one act.

1938–1939 *Season*

SUSANNA, DON'T YOU CRY ("Stephen Foster")   A musical romance in 2 acts by Sarah Newmeyer and Clarence Loomis. Based on melodies of Stephen Foster.

Designed for the American Lyric Theatre in association with the League of Composers. 7 settings. Directed by José Ruben. With the Hall Johnson Choir, directed by Leonard de Paur. Martin Beck Theatre. May 22. (4)

1939–1940

SUMMER NIGHT   A drama in 2 acts by Vicki Baum and Benjamin Glazer.

Designed for Lewis E. Gensler. 7 settings. Directed by Lee Strasberg. With Violet Heming, Lionel Stander, Louis Calhern. St. James Theatre. November 2. (4)

MADAM, WILL YOU WALK   A comedy in 3 acts by Sidney Howard.

Designed for The Playwright's Company. 4 settings. Directed by Margaret Webster. Special music composed and orchestrated by Kurt Weill. With *George M. Cohan,* Peggy Conklin, Sara Allgood, Arthur Kennedy. Out-of-town tryouts during November. Production cancelled.

KINDRED   A play in prologue and 2 acts by Paul Vincent Carroll.

Designed and directed for Edward Choate and Arthur Shields. 2 settings. With Aline MacMahon, Barry Fitzgerald, Arthur Shields, Wallace Ford. Maxine Elliott's Theatre. December 26. (16)

JUNO AND THE PAYCOCK   A play in 3 acts by Sean O'Casey.

Designed for Edward Choate and Arthur Shields, in association with Mr. Jones. 1 setting. Directed by Mr. Shields. With *Barry Fitzgerald, Sara Allgood,* Arthur Shields, Effie Shannon. Mansfield Theatre. January 16. (105) [The first time Sara Allgood and Barry Fitzgerald had appeared together in New York as *Juno* and *"Captain" Boyle,* the roles they had originated in the Dublin production of 1924.]

Contributed to a symposium, "The Theatre Takes Stock," in *Theatre Arts* for May (XXIV: pp. 355–56).

ROMEO AND JULIET   A tragedy by William Shakespeare.

Produced and designed by Laurence Olivier. Lighting by Mr. Jones. Directed by Mr. Olivier and Robert Ross. Scenery and costumes by Motley. Music by Alexander Steinert and Mr. Olivier. With Laurence Olivier, Vivien Leigh, Dame May Whitty, Edmond O'Brien. 51st Street Theatre. May 9. (36)

LOVE FOR LOVE   A comedy in 4 acts by William Congreve.

Designed and directed for The Players' Annual Revival. Costumes by Millia Davenport. Music by Macklin Marrow. Hudson Theatre. Week of June 3. (8)

Device for the American
National Theatre and Academy
1948

During the season, Jones worked on designs for a production of BENJAMIN FRANKLIN, a dramatization by Sidney Howard of Carl Van Doren's 1939 Pulitzer Prize biography, which The Playwrights' Company planned to produce at the end of the season. The plans were cancelled.

TO-NIGHT AT 8:30   Three programs of one-act plays by Noel Coward.

Designed a unit setting for a production given for the benefit of the British War Relief by the British colony in Hollywood at the El Capitan Theatre. The first of the three bills opened on August 5.

Published "Designing a Stage Costume" in *Theatre Arts* for November (XXIV: pp. 791–98); revised and reprinted (1941) as Chapter V in *The Dramatic Imagination.* [Jones's project for a production of PELLÉAS ET MÉLISANDE with marionettes can probably be dated 1940; late in that year he is known to have discussed the subject with Maeterlinck.]

1940–1941 *Season*

On January 14 Jones concluded arrangements to enter under the management of Lee Keedick for a series of lecture tours. Among the colleges and universities which he visited during the next few years were: Brooklyn Institute of Arts and Sciences, Carleton College, Carnegie Institute of Technology, University of Connecticut, Cornell College, Drake University, Fordham University, Iowa State College, University of Kansas City, MacMurray College, University of Minnesota, North Dakota State College, University of Oregon, Stanford University, University of Virginia, Wesleyan University, College of William and Mary, College of Wooster, Yale University.

[In May, 1952, at Harvard University, Jones recorded four of his lectures under the general title, *Towards a New Theatre*. The first lecture, edited by Frederick C. Packard, was released in November, 1955, as a Vocarium Record; the fourth lecture, "Curious and Profitable," had been privately printed by Jones in an undated pamphlet.]

Published "Light and Shadow" in *Theatre Arts* for February (XXV: pp. 131–39); republished as Chapter VI in *The Dramatic Imagination*.

Published "Toward a New Stage" in *Theatre Arts* for March (XXV: pp. 191–200); republished as Chapter VII in *The Dramatic Imagination*.

Published *The Dramatic Imagination: Reflections and Speculations on the Art of the Theatre* (New York: Duell, Sloan, and Pearce, 1941.) [A Japanese translation was published in Tokyo in 1950.]

ORPHEUS, an opera in 3 acts by Gluck.
THE BARBER OF SEVILLE, an opera in 2 acts by Rossini.

> Designed for the Tenth Annual Play Festival of the Central City Opera House Association. Staged by Dr. Herbert Graf. Conducted by Frank St. Leger. [THE BARBER OF SEVILLE: 3 settings, 14 performances; ORPHEUS: 5 settings, 11 performances. Both operas sung in English.] Central City Opera House, Central City, Colorado. July 5–26.

> During 1941 Jones worked as a project on designs for a production of RICHARD III with a unit setting and projected effects.

> Death of Mrs. Jones, August 1, at Greenwich, Connecticut.

WITHOUT LOVE   A comedy in 3 acts by Philip Barry.

> Designed for The Theatre Guild, Inc. 1 setting. Directed by Robert B. Sinclair and Arthur Hopkins. Incidental music by Richard E. Myers. With Katharine Hepburn, Elliott Nugent. St. James Theatre. November 10. (113)

> During 1942 Jones designed as projects: Paul Vincent Carroll's THE OLD FOOLISHNESS: *Act II, A ruined castle in Ireland;* and, by an unknown author, THE LORDS OF THE WEST: *Act III, A battlemented fortress.*

THE CRUCIFIXION OF CHRIST   A stage version by Leopold Stokowski of *The St. Matthew Passion* of J. S. Bach.

> Designed for a benefit performance for the American Friends Service Committee. Conducted by Leopold Stokowski. Soloists: Jennie Tourel, Eleanor Steber, Glenn Darwin, Gerhard Pechner, Lucius Metz. Choreography by George Balanchine. With Lillian Gish and a cast of mimes from the American Ballet School; the Collegiate Chorale conducted by Robert Shaw; and players from several student orchestras. Metropolitan Opera House. April 9. (1)

Published "Filled and Pervaded" in *The New Republic* for June 21 (CVIII: p. 829). [A review of an exhibition of paintings by Stark Young.]

1943–1944

OTHELLO

A tragedy by William Shakespeare, adapted to 2 acts and 8 scenes by Margaret Webster.

Designed for The Theatre Guild, Inc., in association with John Haggott. Variations of a unit setting. Directed by Miss Webster. Music by Tom Bennett. [With Paul Robeson as *Othello,* José Ferrer as *Iago,* Uta Hagen as *Desdemona,* Margaret Webster as *Emilia.*] Shubert Theatre. October 19. (296)

JACKPOT

A musical comedy in 2 acts by Guy Bolton, Sidney Sheldon, and Ben Roberts. Music and lyrics by Howard Dietz and Vernon Duke.

Designed with Raymond Sovey for Vinton Freedley. Costumes by Kiviette. Staged by Roy Hargrave. Dances by Lauretta Jefferson. Ballet directed by Charles Weidman. Music directed by Max Meth. With *Allan Jones,* Jerry Lester, Benny Baker, Nanette Fabray, Mary Wickes, Betty Garrett. Alvin Theatre. January 13. (69)

HELEN GOES TO TROY

An operetta in 2 acts by Gottfried Reinhardt and John Meehan, Jr. Lyrics by Herbert Baker. Music by Erich Wolfgang Korngold. Based on Max Reinhardt's version of Jacques Offenbach's LA BELLE HÉLÈNE.

Designed for Yolanda Mero-Irion, producing for the New Opera Company. Costumes by Ladislas Czettel. Staged by Herbert Graf. Choreography by Leonide Massine. Dialogue directed by Melville Cooper. With *Jarmila Novotna,* Ernest Truex. Alvin Theatre. April 24. (97)

1944–1945

THE CHILDREN'S CHRISTMAS STORY

A production conceived by Leopold Stokowski.

Designed for the New York City Symphony. Narration of Biblical events by Augustin Duncan. Pantomime by 55 New York City school children, with the Collegiate Chorale directed by Robert Shaw. Lighting by Hans Sondheimer. New York City Center. December 21, 23, 24. (3)

During 1944, Jones prepared a series of designs for a production by Billy Rose of Shakespeare's HENRY VIII. Plans for the production were cancelled.

Published "Nijinsky and *Til Eulenspiegel*" in *Dance Index* for April (I: pp. 44–54). [Jones had hoped to publish a book on four great artists of the theatre; in addition to "The Gloves of Isadora" and this article on Nijinsky, it was to have included essays on Sarah Bernhardt and John Barrymore.]

Exhibited 60 stage designs and 2 panels of sketches for LA CUCARACHA and BECKY SHARP in a one-man show at the Museum of Modern Art, April 11–June 24.

LUTE SONG

A love story with music in 3 acts and 17 scenes by Sidney Howard and Will Irwin. Adapted from the popular Chinese classic, PI-PA-KI. Music by Raymond Scott. Lyrics by Bernard Hanighen.

1945–1946

Designed for Michael Myerberg. Directed by John Houseman. With *Mary Martin*, Yul Brynner, McKay Morris, Helen Craig, Clarence Derwent, Augustin Duncan, Rex O'Malley, Mildred Dunnock, Ralph Clanton. Choreography by Yeichi Nimura. Musical director, Eugene Kusmiak. Plymouth Theatre. February 6. (142)

THE ICEMAN COMETH   A drama in 4 acts by Eugene O'Neill.

1946–1947

Designed for The Theatre Guild, Inc., in association with Armina Marshall. 2 settings. Directed by Eddie Dowling. [With James Barton as *Hickey*, Dudley Digges as *Harry Hope*.] Martin Beck Theatre. October 9. (136)

1946–1947 *Season*

During 1945 Jones worked on preliminary sketches for Robert Whitehead and Oliver Rea's production with Judith Anderson of Robinson Jeffers' adaptation of the MEDEA of Euripides; later he withdrew from the production. He also designed as projects a setting for O'Neill's A TOUCH OF THE POET, and the Sleepwalking Scene from Shakespeare's MACBETH. (At an earlier date, Jones designed another version of the Sleepwalking Scene for a revival of the play with Jane Cowl by The Players, but plans for the production were cancelled and I have been unable to determine when they were being considered.)

A MOON FOR THE MISBEGOTTEN   A play in 4 acts by Eugene O'Neill.

Designed for The Theatre Guild, Inc. 2 settings. Directed by Arthur Shields. With James Dunn, J. M. Kerrigan, Mary Welch. Pre-Broadway tryout opened in Columbus, Ohio, on February 20. Closed on March 29 in St. Louis, after playing Cleveland, Detroit, and Pittsburgh. Production then cancelled.

1947–1948

Published "The Gloves of Isadora" in *Theatre Arts* for October (XXXI, pp. 17–22).

1949 : *Summer*

OUT OF DUST   A play in 2 acts by Lynn Riggs.

Designed for The Theatre Guild, Inc. Directed by Mary Hunter. With Helen Craig, Billy Redfield, Berry Kroeger, Joan Lorring, Edwin Jerome. Westport Country Playhouse, Westport, Connecticut. August 8–13.

1949–1950

THE ENCHANTED   A comedy in 3 acts by Jean Giraudoux. Adapted by Maurice Valency.

Designed for David Lowe and Richard Davidson. 2 settings. Directed by George S. Kaufman. Music by Francis Poulenc. Dances by Jean Erdman. Lyceum Theatre. January 18. (45)

Represented in an exhibition presented by the Harvard Theatre Collection, in co-operation with the Fogg Art Museum: *Three Designers for the Contemporary Theatre, Robert Edmond Jones '10, Donald Oenslager '23, Lee Simonson '09.* Fogg Art Museum, Harvard University. October 16–November 25.

1950–1951 *Season*

THE FLYING DUTCHMAN   A romantic opera in 3 acts by Richard Wagner.

Designed from sketches by Jones for the Metropolitan Opera Association by Charles Elson. 3 settings. Costumes designed by Mary Percy Schenck. Staged by Herbert Graf. Conducted by Fritz Reiner. [With Hans Hotter making his Metropolitan début as *The Dutchman.*] Metropolitan Opera House. November 9. (7)

THE GREEN PASTURES *(Revival)*

Designed for The Wigreen Company, in association with Harry Fromkes. Directed by Marc Connelly. Broadway Theatre. March 15. (44) [The 1930 production, in New York and on tour, had played a total of 1,642 performances.]

[The revival of THE GREEN PASTURES represented the close of Jones's professional career. After a long period of illness, he died on November 26, 1954, in Milton, New Hampshire.]

1954

Self-caricature
1954

ON SUNDAY afternoon, December 12, 1954, a simple memorial meeting was held in New York at the Plymouth Theatre. Jo Mielziner introduced the various speakers. Walter Abel read a letter from Kenneth Macgowan who was in California. Walter Hampden read Jones's Preface to *Drawings for the Theatre.* Brian Aherne and John Mason Brown spoke of their personal memories of Bobby Jones. And then, after a brief ceremony which included music from Gluck's ORPHEUS, the curtain of the Plymouth Theatre—very, very slowly—was lowered.

The tailpiece on page 167 is reproduced through courtesy of the publisher, Farrar & Rinehart, Inc., New York; the ANTA device through courtesy of the American National Theatre and Academy. The balance of the decorations throughout the Chronology first appeared in *Theatre Arts Magazine* and *Theatre Arts Monthly*, and are reproduced by permission.

L'ENVOI

"P<small>ERCHANCE TO DREAM</small>," said Hamlet. "Did you ever see a dream walking?" asked the Broadway song of many years ago. References to the word "dream," singular and plural and with its derivatives, are spread over some two and a half columns of the new centennial edition of Bartlett. And why not? Sleeping men are most awake and waking men most alive when they dream.

Bobby Jones was a magnificent dreamer whose genius it was to transmute his dreams into reality, thus making it possible for others to share them. The splendor of the vision which fired his imagination was as luminously present when he talked or wrote about the theatre as when he worked for it. He was not a stage designer; he was a scenic artist. More accurately, he was an artist of uncommon gifts whose medium was the stage. This is why his contributions to so ephemeral a form of expression possess abiding incandescence.

For all too many people the theatre is the equivalent of "a night off." It never was to Bobby. To him it was "a night on." It was always in his phrase "an exceptional occasion," when perceptions were alerted, when life took on new dimensions, when hearts were lifted by excitement, and eyes—even though confronted with the squalid—feasted on splendor.

"Lustrous" was a favorite word of Bobby's, and "lustrous," of all the possible adjectives evoked by his settings and sketches, is the one which most accurately describes their quality. He did not have to have a palace as his assignment in order to create beauty. A barroom became beautiful when seen through his eyes. The beauty he created was never sentimental, vapid, or self-advertising in its prettiness. It had the dignity that comes from a fine sense of selection, the strength of simple emphasis, and a purity of design that gave glory to daily things.

His settings were not reproductions of reality. They were extensions of it. They had exaltation in them, too. Although the mood and meaning of a play lived in them, they lived a life of their own. This is why Bobby's sketches have outlasted the productions for which they were made and will continue to do so. The dream that was his walks in them, as summoning as ever, and the more welcome and needed in today's almost dreamless theatre, as reminders of what the theatre can be.

A FOOTNOTE TO THIS EDITION

DURING the twenty years since the first publication of this book, in 1958, at least half of the original designs, from which the full-page plates were made, have changed ownership. A list of the new owners follows. It may not be complete, but it includes all instances of which we have been informed.

HARVARD THEATRE COLLECTION   *Birthday of the Infanta,* page 34
Richard III, page 36
Hamlet, page 46
Much Ado About Nothing, page 58
Camille, pages 86 and 88
Pelléas et Mélisande, page 96

MR. JOHN HUSTON   *Desire Under the Elms,* page 54

MR. EDWARD F. KOOK   *Hamlet,* page 48
The Fountain, page 56

MR. JO MIELZINER   *Redemption,* page 32
Machinal, page 68

MR. DONALD O. OENSLAGER   *Macbeth,* page 126

MR. ROBERT L. THIRKIELD   *Macbeth,* pages 38 and 40

WESLEYAN UNIVERSITY THEATRE DEPARTMENT
Henry VIII, pages 108, 110, 112, and 114
A Touch of the Poet, page 124

YALE DRAMA SCHOOL   *Pelléas et Mélisande,* page 44
La Gioconda, page 64
The Green Pastures, pages 72, 74, and 76

Middletown, Connecticut   RALPH PENDLETON
June 1977

INDEX OF PRODUCTIONS

IN ADDITION to the projects and productions of Robert Edmond Jones, the index lists authors, translators, adapters, composers, choreographers, and producers. References to full-page plates are indicated by italics.

Ah, Wilderness!: 172
Akins, Zoë: 151, 154, 157
Allen, Frank: 149
All God's Chillun Got Wings: 159
American Laboratory Theatre: 164
American Lyric Theatre: 175, 176
American Opera Company: *66, 70*, 165, 167
Ancient Mariner, The: 141, 158
Andersen, Hans Christian: 151
Anderson, Maxwell: *84*, 161, 170, 172
Anderson, Sherwood: 160
Anna Christie: 154
As You Like It: 162
At the Gateway: *52*, 158

Bach, Johann Sebastian: 179
Baker, Herbert: 180
Barber of Seville, The: *98*, 179
Barnhart, Harry: 152
Barry, Philip: *15, 94*, 163, 165, 166, 173, 175, 179
Baum, Vicki: 176
Be Calm, Camilla: 151
Bechhofer, C. E.: 148
Becky Sharp: (film) 143, 173, 181; (play) 166
Beggars of Life: 161
Behrman, S. N.: *15*, 166

Belle Hélène, La: 180
Benelli, Sem: 152, 162
Benét, Stephen Vincent: 175
Benjamin Franklin: 177
Berg, Alban: 169
Berger, Henning: 149
Berkeley, Reginald: 170
Bernard, Jean-Jacques: 164
Bernstein, Henri: 154
Beyond: 160
Birthday of the Infanta, The: xiii, 3, 4-5, 6, *34*, 152
Bizet, Georges: 171
Björkman, Edwin: 157
Blackwell, Donald: 172
Blau, Bela, Inc.: 167, 175
Bloch, Bertram: 173
Blok, Alexander: 162
Bolton, Guy: 180
Boule de Suif: 167
Boyce, Neith: 147
Bradford, Roark: 168
Brady, William A., Jr.: 163
Brewer, George, Jr.: 173

BRIDE OF THE LAMB: 164
Bromfield, Louis: *62*, 164
BUCCANEER, THE: 22, 161
Büchner, Georg: 169

CALIBAN BY THE YELLOW SANDS: 18, 148, 149
CAMILLE: *86, 88*, 170, 171
CARMEN: 171
Carmi, Maria: *52*
Carpenter, John Alden: *34, 60*, 152, 164
Carroll, Paul Vincent: *104*, 176, 179
CENA DELLE BEFFE, LA: 152, 162
CENCI, THE: 22, *28*, 146, 153
CENTRAL CITY NIGHTS: 174
Central City Opera House Association: 15, *86, 88, 98*, 170,
    172, 173, 174, 175, 179
CHANNEL ROAD, THE: 167
Chappell, Delos: 170, 171
Chappell, Edna: 170
Chekhov, Anton: 175
Chicago Opera Association: *34*, 152
CHILDREN OF DARKNESS: 168
CHILDREN'S CHRISTMAS STORY, THE: 180
Choate, Edward: 176
CLAW, THE: 154
Clugston, Katharine: 166
Cocteau, Jean: *80*, 169
Coleridge, Samuel Taylor: 158
Colton, John: 172
Congreve, William: 142, 160, 177
Connelly, Marc: 72, *74, 76*, 167, 168, 175
CONSTANCY: 147
Cook, George Cram: 147
Cornell, Katharine: 171
Coward, Noel: 177

Cowl, Jane: *128*, 182
CRIME IN THE WHISTLER ROOM, THE: 159
CROSS ROADS: 167
CRUCIFIXION OF CHRIST, THE: 179
CUCARACHA, LA: 143, 173, 181

DADDY'S GONE A-HUNTING: 154
Damrosch, Gretchen: 170
DANCING PIRATE, THE: 143, 174
Danielou, Jean: 169
D'Annunzio, Gabriele: *64*, 165
DARK VICTORY: 173
Davidson, Richard: 182
Davis, J. Frank: 170
Debussy, Claude: *44*, 151, 155
DELUGE, THE: 149, 155
DESIRE UNDER THE ELMS: 8, *54*, 141, 160
DEVIL AND DANIEL WEBSTER, THE: 175
DEVIL'S GARDEN, THE: 147
Diaghileff, Serge: 148
Dietz, Howard: 180
DIFF'RENT: 160
Duke, Vernon: 180
Dumas, Alexandre, fils: *86, 88*, 170
Du Maurier, George: 151
Duncan, Augustin: 155
Dunn, Edward Delaney: 154
Dunsany, Lord: 147

Ellis, Edith: 147
EMPEROR JONES, THE: 158
ENCHANTED, THE: 182
ENCHANTMENT: 171
Equity Players, Inc.: 159
Euripides: 182
EVERGREEN TREE, THE: 150
EVERYWHERE I ROAM: 175
Evreinov, Nicholas: 148

Experimental Theatre, Inc.: *54*, 157, 158, 159, 160, 161

FANNY'S FIRST PLAY: 151
Faragon, Francis Edward: 173, 174
Farrar and Rinehart, Inc.: 72, *74, 76*
FASHION: 15, 141, 142, 157
FAUST: *66*, 165
Flavin, Martin: 167
FLYING DUTCHMAN, THE: 183
Foster, Stephen: 176
FOUNTAIN, THE: *56*, 141, 163
France, Anatole: *30*, 147
Freedley, Vinton: 180
Fromkes, Harry: 183

Galsworthy, John: 152
GAOLER'S WENCH, THE: 168
GARDEN OF PARADISE, THE: 151
Gensler, Lewis E.: 166, 167, 176
GENTILE WIFE, THE: 151
GEORGE DANDIN: 158
GEORGE WASHINGTON: 153
Gilbert, W. S.: 160
GIOCONDA, LA: *64*, 165
Giordano, Umberto: 162
Giraud, Albert: 171
Giraudoux, Jean: 182
Glaspell, Susan: 147
Glazer, Benjamin: 176
GLITTERING GATE, THE: 147
Gluck, Christoph Willibald: 179
GLÜCKLICHE HAND, DIE: 168
Goethe, Johann Wolfgang von: 165
Goldberg, Isaac: 155
GOOD GRACIOUS ANNABELLE: 149
Gordon, Max: *90, 92*, 174
Gounod, Charles: *66*, 165
GRANNY MAUMEE: 149

Granville-Barker, Harley: *30*, 147
Grayson, David: 151
GREAT GOD BROWN, THE: 142, 163
GREEN BAY TREE, THE: 172
Green Bay Tree, The: 164
GREEN PASTURES, THE: 6, 15, 72, *74, 76*, 167, 168, 183
Grossman, Samuel S.: 154
Group Theatre, Inc.: *84*, 170
GUIBOUR: 151

Haggart, John D.: 167
Haggott, John: 180
HAIRY APE, THE: 155
HAMLET: 15, 20, *46, 48*, 156
Hampden, Walter: 153
HAND OF FATE, THE: 168
Hanighen, Bernard: 181
Hapgood, Emilie: 149, 162
HAPPY ENDING, THE: 148
Harris, Jed: 166, 172
Harris, Ray: 174
Hart, Lorenz: 174
Hartleben, Erich: 171
Hasenclever, Walter: 160
Hauptmann, Gerhart: 156
HEAVENLY AND EARTHLY LOVE: 157
HEDDA GABLER: 16, 24, 150, 159
HELEN GOES TO TROY: 180
HEMPFIELD: 151
HENRY IV: 157
HENRY VI: 153
HENRY VIII: 17, *108, 110, 112, 114*, 181
Hewes, Margaret: 172
Hirshbein, Peretz: 155
HOLIDAY: 166

Hooker, Brian: 157, 175
Hopkins, Arthur: 24, 25, 32, 36, 38, *40, 46, 48, 62, 68*, 147, 148, 149, 150, 151, 152, 153, 154, 155, 156, 157, 161, 162, 163, 165, 166, 167, 168, 170, 173
Hopkins, Charles: 167
HOUSE OF WOMEN, THE: *62*, 164
Howard, Sidney: *42, 116, 118, 120*, 133, 154, 155, 162, 165, 176, 177, 181
Hughes, Hatcher: 161
Hugo, Victor: 175
Hurlbut, William J: 164

Ibsen, Henrik: 150, 159, 163, 169
ICEMAN COMETH, THE: 15, *122*, 181
IDEAL HUSBAND, AN: 151
IDLE INN, THE: 155
IN A GARDEN: 163
Ingster, Boris: 174
INTERIOR: 147
Irwin, Will: *116, 118, 120*, 133, 135, 181

JACKPOT: 180
Janney, Russell: 151, 162
Jeffers, Robinson: 182
JEST, THE: 15, 152, 162, 163
Jones, Robert Edmond: (as adapter) 170; (as director) 141–2, 149, 157, 158, 159, 160, 161, 163, 170, 171, 172, 173, 174, 175, 176, 177; (as film designer) 142–3, 173, 174; (as producer) *56*, 141–2, 157, 158, 161, 162, 163, 164, 170, 172, 173, 174, 175, 176. *See also* Experimental Theatre, Inc.
JOYOUS SEASON, THE: 173
JUNO AND THE PAYCOCK: 176

Kaufman, George S.: 167
KINDRED: 176
KINGDOM OF SANCHO PANZA, THE: *50*, 162
Korngold, Erich Wolfgang: 180
Kummer, Clare: 15, 149, 150, 151, 155

LADDER, THE: 170
LADIES LEAVE: 167
"Lady of Quality, A": 166
LADY WITH A LAMP, THE: 170
Lange, Sven: 154
LAST NIGHT OF DON JUAN, THE: 162
Lattuada, Felice: *78*, 169
LAUGHING LADY, THE: 156
LAUNZI: 157
League of Composers: *80*, 168, 169, 171, 175, 176
Lehar, Franz: 172
Lengyel, Melchior: *50*, 162
Lewissohn, Ludwig: 156
Liszt, Franz: 149
LITTLE EYOLF: 163
Little Mermaid, The: 151
LITTLE SHEPHERD, THE: 151
LIVING CORPSE, THE: 151
LIVING MASK, THE: 157
Livingston, Arthur: 157
Loomis, Clarence: *70*, 167, 176
LORDS OF THE WEST, THE: *106*, 179
LOVE FOR LOVE: 15, 141, 160, 161, 177
LOVERS, THE: 154
Lowe, David: 182
LUCRECE: 6, 171
LUTE SONG: 18, *116, 118, 120*, 132–138, 181

MacArthur, Charles: 165
MACBETH: xiii, 3, 5–6, 15, *38, 40, 126, 128*, 154, 182
McCarthy, Lillah: 147
MacDonald, Anna Sprague: 151

Macgowan, Kenneth: *56*, 146, 155, 156, 157, 158, 161, 162, 163, 164, 168, 170. *See also* Experimental Theatre, Inc. and pp. 139–143

MACHINAL: *68*, 165

McKaig, Alexander: 173

Mackaye, Percy: 148, 150, 152, 153

Macpherson, Jean and La du Rocher: 148

MADAM, WILL YOU WALK: 176

Maeterlinck, Maurice: *44, 96*, 147, 153, 155, 177

MAGICAL CITY, THE: 151

MAN WHO MARRIED A DUMB WIFE, THE: 7, 15, 24, *30*, 131, 147

Marshall, Armina: 181

MARTINE: 164

MARY OF SCOTLAND: 172

Matthias, Rita: 160

Maupassant, Guy de: 167

Maxwell, William B.: 147

Mayer, Edwin Justus: 168

MEDEA: 182

Meehan, John, Jr.: 180

MEPHISTO WALTZ: 148

MERCHANT OF VENICE, THE: 146

Mero-Irion, Yolanda: 180

MERRY DEATH, THE: 148

MERRY WIDOW, THE: 172

Metropolitan Opera Association: *60, 78*, 148, 162, 164, 169, 183

MICHEL AUCLAIR: 141, 160

Miles, Carlton: 172

Miles, William: 172

Millay, Edna St. Vincent: 157

Milton, Robert: 164

Mitchell, Langdon: 166, 173

Molière: *78*, 158, 169

Molnar, Ferenc: 157

MOON FOR THE MISBEGOTTEN, A: 182

Moore, Douglas: 175

Moses, Harry: 171

MOUNTAIN MAN, THE: 155

MOURNING BECOMES ELECTRA: 15, *82*, 170

Mowatt, Anna Cora: 157

MR. MONEYPENNY: 166

MUCH ADO ABOUT NOTHING: *58*, 153, 163, 170

Myerberg, Michael: *116, 118, 120*, 133, 134, 181

Neighborhood Playhouse: 151

Newmeyer, Sarah: 176

New Opera Company: 180

New York City Symphony: 180

NIGHT OVER TAOS: *84*, 170

Nijinski, Vaslav: 148–149

NINE PINE STREET: 172

Obey, André: 171

O'Casey, Sean: 176

OEDIPUS REX: *80*, 169, 170

Offenbach, Jacques: 180

OLD FOOLISHNESS, THE: *104*, 179

Olivier, Laurence: 177

Ol' Man Adam an' His Chillun: 6, 168

O'Neil, Raymond: 160

O'Neill, Eugene: (as author) 15, 17, *54, 56, 82, 122, 124*, 141, 154, 155, 158, 159, 160, 163, 170, 172, 181, 182; (as producer) *56*, 141, 157, 158, 161, 162, 163, 164. *See also* Experimental Theatre, Inc.

ORPHEUS: 179

OTHELLO: 18, *90, 92*, 173, 174, 180

OUT OF DUST: 182

OUTSIDE LOOKING IN: 161

Page, Curtis Hidden: 147

PARIS BOUND: 165

Parker, Austin: 167
PASSING PRESENT, THE: 170
PATIENCE: 132, 141, 160
PELLÉAS ET MÉLISANDE: *44, 96*, 155, 177
Pemberton, Brock: *42*, 154, 157, 167
Philadelphia Grand Opera Company: 169
Philadelphia Opera Association: 168
Philadelphia Orchestra: *80*, 169
PHILADELPHIA STORY, THE: *94*, 175
PIERROT LUNAIRE: 171
PILGRIMAGE, THE: 163
Pinero, Sir Arthur Wing: 161
Pioneer Pictures: 143, 173, 174
PI-PA-KI: 133, 134, 181
Pirandello, Luigi: 52, 157, 158
Players Club: 161, 166, 177, 182
Playwrights' Company: 176, 177
Pollock, Channing: 166
PRÉCIEUSES RIDICULES, LES: *78*, 169
PREZIOSE RIDICOLE, LE: *78*, 169
Provincetown Players: 147, 155, 157, 158, 160
Purcell, Gertrude: 156

Radio City Music Hall: 15, 145, 171
Rea, Oliver: 182
REBOUND: 168
Red Cross, American: 149, 150
REDEMPTION: 24, 32, 151
Reed, Joseph Verner: 168, 170
Reinhardt, Gottfried: 180
Reinhardt, Max: 7, 14, 146, 180
RESCUING ANGEL, THE: 150
Rice, Cale Young: *70*, 167
Rice, Elmer: 166
RICHARD III: 15, 18, 24, *36, 100, 102*, 153, 179

RIDER OF DREAMS, THE: 149
Riggs, Lynn: 168, 182
Rivers, Laurence, Inc.: 168
ROADSIDE: 168
Roberts, Ben: 180
Rodgers, Richard: 174
ROLL CALL, THE: 150
ROMEO AND JULIET: 156, 177
ROSE BERND: 156
Rose, Billy: *108, 110, 112, 114*, 181
Rossato, Arturo: *78*, 169
Rossini, Gioacchino: *98*, 179
Rostand, Edmond: 162
ROYAL FANDANGO, A: 157
RUINT: 161
RUY BLAS: 175

SABRINA: 152
SAINT, THE: 159
St. Matthew Passion, The: 179
SALOMÉ: 13
SALVATION: 165
SAMSON AND DELILAH: 154
SANCHO PANZA: 162
Schönberg, Arnold: 168, 171
Scott, Raymond: 181
SEA GULL, THE: 175
SEE NAPLES AND DIE: 166
SERENA BLANDISH: 166
SEVEN PRINCESSES, THE: 153
SEVEN YEAR LOVE: 167
Shairp, Mordaunt: 172
Shakespeare Tercentenary: 148
Shakespeare, William: *36, 38, 40, 46, 48, 58, 90, 92, 100, 102, 108, 110, 112, 114, 126, 128*, 153, 154, 156, 162, 163, 173, 174, 177, 179, 180, 181, 182
Shaw, Bernard: 151
Sheldon, Edward: 151, 152

Sheldon, Sidney: 180
Shelley, Percy Bysshe: *28, 146*
Shields, Arthur: 176
SHOW BOOTH, THE: 162
Shubert, Lee: 172
Simon, Robert A.: 165
SIMON THE CYRENIAN: 149
SKYSCRAPERS: End papers, 15, *60*, 164
SONG OF ROLAND, THE: 154
Sophocles: 169
SPOOK SONATA, THE: 141, 157
Squier, Emma-Lindsay: 174
S. S. GLENCAIRN: 159
S. S. TENACITY, THE: 155
Stage Society of New York: 146, 147
Stallings, Laurence: 161
STAR, THE: 162
STEPHEN FOSTER: 176
Stewart, Donald Ogden: 168
Stokowski, Leopold: *80*, 169, 179, 180
Strauss, Richard: 148
Stravinsky, Igor: *80*, 169
STRIFE: 152
Strindberg, August: 141, 157
SUCCESSFUL CALAMITY, A: 149
Sullivan, Arthur: 160
SUMMER NIGHT: 176
Sundgaard, Arnold: 175
SUPPRESSED DESIRES: 147
SUSANNA, DON'T YOU CRY: 176
Sutro, Alfred: 156
SWORDS: *42*, 154

Taylor, Deems: 157
Taylor, Laurette: 171
Taylor, Leila: 156
Thackeray, William Makepeace: 166, 173
Thayer, Sigourney: 163

Theatre Guild, Inc: 58, 82, 94, *122*, 147, 163, 170, 172, 175, 179, 180, 181, 182
THESE DAYS: 166
Thompson, Charlotte: 151
TIL EULENSPIEGEL: 15, 24, 148, 149
Tolstoi, Leo: *32*, 151
TO-NIGHT AT 8:30: 177
Torrence, Ridgely: 149
TOUCH OF THE POET, A: *124*, 182
Treadwell, Sophie: *68*, 165, 167
TRELAWNEY OF "THE WELLS": 161
TRILBY: 151
TRIUMPH OF THE EGG, THE: 160
Tully, Jim: 161

Valency, Maurice: 182
Van Doren, Carl: 177
Vanity Fair: 166, 173
Vildrac, Charles: 155, 160, 163
VIOL DE LUCRÈCE, LE: 171
VOLTAIRE: 156

Wagner, Charles L.: 155
Wagner, Jack: 174
Wagner, Richard: 183
Washington Square Players: 147, 148
Webster, Margaret: 180
WEEK-END: 167
WELDED: 158
Wellman, Rita: 151
WHEN WE DEAD AWAKEN: 169
Whitehead, Robert: 182
Wigreen Company: 183
WILD DUCK, THE: 150
Wilde, Oscar: 151, 152

Wilder, Thornton: 171
WILL OF SONG, THE: 152
Wilson, Edmund: 159
Wiman, Dwight Deere: 163
WITHOUT LOVE: 179
Wolheim, Louis: 154, 155
Woollcott, Alexander: 167

WOZZECK: 169

YOLANDA OF CYPRUS: *70*, 167
Young, Stark: 158, 159, 175. *See also* pp. 3–6.

Ziegfeld, Florenz, Jr.: 150